*After Every War*

FACING PAGES | FACING PAGES

NICHOLAS JENKINS
*Series Editor*

HORACE, THE ODES
New Translations by Contemporary Poets,
*edited by J. D. McClatchy*

HOTHOUSES
Poems 1889,
by Maurice Maeterlinck,
*translated by Richard Howard*

LANDSCAPE WITH ROWERS
Poetry from the Netherlands,
*translated and introduced by J. M. Coetzee*

AFTER EVERY WAR
Twentieth-Century Women Poets,
*translated from the German by Eavan Boland*

# After Every War

Twentieth-Century Women Poets

*Translations from the German*

*by Eavan Boland*

PRINCETON
UNIVERSITY
PRESS

*Princeton & Oxford*

Published by Princeton University Press, 41 William Street, Princeton, New Jersey 08540

In the United Kingdom: Princeton University Press, 3 Market Place, Woodstock, Oxfordshire OX20 1SY

All Rights Reserved

LIBRARY OF CONGRESS CATALOGING-IN-PUBLICATION DATA

After every war : twentieth-century women poets / translations from the German by Eavan Boland.
     p.    cm. — (Facing pages)
    Includes bibliographical references and index.
    ISBN 0-691-11745-4 (alk. paper)
    1. German poetry—20th century—Translations into English.  2. German poetry—Women authors—Translations into English.  I. Boland, Eavan. II. Series.
PT1156.A38 2004
831'.910809287—dc22     2003061014

British Library Cataloging-in-Publication Data is available

This book has been composed in Electra LH

Printed on acid-free paper. ∞

www.pupress.princeton.edu

Printed in the United States of America

10  9  8  7  6  5  4  3  2  1

The author acknowledges the following publishers for permission to translate from the German: Rose Ausländer: © S. Fischer Verlag GmbH, Frankfurt am Main 1990; Elisabeth Langgässer: er, Geist in den Sinnen behaust. © Matthias-Grünewald-Verlag, Mainz 1951, Germany; Nelly Sachs: © Suhrkamp Verlag, Frankfurt am Main 1961; Gertrud Kolmar: © Suhrkamp Verlag Frankfurt am Main 1983; Else Lasker-Schüler: © Suhrkamp Verlag Frankfurt am Main 1996; Ingeborg Bachmann ©Piper Verlag and Zephyr Press (U.S.); Marie Luise Kaschnitz: © Cassen Verlag, München, Germany; Hilde Domin: © 1987 S. Fischer Verlag GmbH Frankfurt am Main; Dagmar Nick: © Rimbaud Verlag. For photographs of the poets, the author gratefully acknowledges: S. Fischer Verlag (Rose Ausländer); Schiller-Nationalmuseum Deutsches Literaturarchiv (Elisabeth Langgässer); Suhrkamp Verlag (Nelly Sachs); Schiller-Nationalmuseum Deutsches Literaturarchiv (Gertrud Kolmar); Suhrkamp Verlag (Else Lasker-Schüler); Renate von Mangoldt (Ingeborg Bachmann); Suhrkamp Verlag (Marie Luise Kaschnitz); S. Fischer Verlag (Hilde Domin); and Peter Peitsch/peitschophoto.com (Dagmar Nick).

TO THE MEMORY OF MY MOTHER

*and her friendship with the Burghartz family*

*After every war somebody must clean up*

WISŁAWA SZYMBORSKA

# CONTENTS

DAGMAR NICK (b. 1926)

---

*Author Key to Map*

Ausländer: b Czernowitz, 1901, d Dusseldorf, 1988

Langgässer: b Alzey, 1899, d Karlsruhe, 1950

Sachs: b Berlin, 1891, d Stockholm, 1970

Kolmar: b Berlin, 1894, d Auschwitz, 1943

Lasker-Schüler: b Elberfeld, 1869, d Jerusalem, 1945

Bachmann: b Klagenfurt, 1926, d Rome, 1973

Kaschnitz: b Karlsruhe, 1901, d Rome, 1974

Domin: b Cologne, 1909, lives Heidelberg

Nick: b Breslau, 1926, lives Munich

# PLACES OF ORIGIN

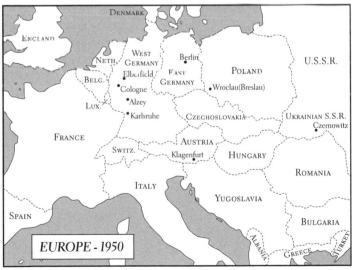

*After Every War*

# INTRODUCTION

## I

When I was a child two German girls came to help my mother in the house. It was just after the war. The small towns of Germany were in the grip of winter, hunger, and disgrace. These girls, who were sisters, hardly more than teenagers, had left that aftermath behind and come to the shelter of a country which had been neutral. There was rationing in Ireland. But there was also butter and meat. Clothing was plentiful. It was an easier place to be.

I was too young to remember their actual arrival. They came into my consciousness with my first words, my first memories. I remember the kitchen, the damp clothes, the snap of the fire, the smell of peat. I remember one of them opening a door that led into the darkness of a back lane. I can hear their voices as they folded clothes and put away plates. I can hear my own voice as I said back the numbers they tried to teach me: *eins zwei drei vier fünf*. Over and over again. Or the quick phrases I learned because they spoke the reality of their lives. *Ich bin beschäftigt*. I am busy.

Above all, I remember that when my parents left the room, and there was no need to learn or be polite, they spoke to each other in rapid, headlong sentences, shutting out with relief the Irish twilight, the small child, and all the evidence of what was not home.

For many years they were a background memory. Gradually,

that changed. They became at once clearer and more mysterious: intaglios, cut deeper in my consciousness than I had realized. Even their voices began to return. What was it I had heard? Gossip and anecdote? Or was I hearing distant towns, in their harsh moment of reckoning—and wider tragedies of nationhood and inhumanity—creeping through their words like fog under a windowsill?

The truth is I couldn't know: not then, not now. But some of the yearning and curiosity I still feel about them is in this book. It is the outcome of years of retrospection and regret, of knowing I had not asked them the questions I later wanted to ask. When I first saw them they were teenagers, sisters. Both are now dead.

But later it seemed that the door one of them opened was legendary, not real—that it led from our ordinary, teatime kitchen into the very heart of a broken Europe. And the conduit, the path was language. A language I could not understand but which spoke to me all the same.

It still speaks to me—that language I cannot understand but need to hear. And that, I think, covers some of the paradox of translation. Some of the poems in this book were being written, or had been written, at the very moment those sisters were talking. In some of these lines their loneliness, their necessary absence is explained far more clearly than they or I could then have managed.

## II

There are nine poets in this book. Their dates of birth range from the mid-nineteenth century to the first decades of the twentieth. All are German-speaking. Their places of origin are from as far north as Bukowina and as far south as Carinthia. Their places of exile range from Sweden to South America.

All wrote in the presence or aftermath of a war which cut deeply into their lives. Of course, they lived different lives and experienced the war variously. It also needs to be remembered that the poems here are only a fraction, albeit an important fraction, of the work written by these poets.

These are poems, then, written in the shadow of a war. But there is more to it than that. They are poems written by those whom war injures and excludes in a particular way—in other words, women. Nevertheless, the question may persist: why women, why war? If these look like restrictive categories for translation, there is a reason.

The problem with human catastrophe is that it can be remembered all too well. But it is much harder to re-imagine it. What brings it from the domain of fact to the realm of feeling is often just a detail. A cup, a shoe, an open window, a village roof with missing slates. Once we see it, we recognize it. *That could have been me,* we suddenly think. *I could have been there.* That moment of private truth, simply because it cuts history down to size, has a rare value.

It seems to me there is something compelling and revealing in the way the world of the public poet encounters the hidden life of the woman in these poems. As it does so, both change. The individual experience of the first makes the collective experience of the second available in a new and poignant way. The result is a dark, moving interplay of determinism and elegy.


## III

That in itself, however, requires a word of warning. These are not war poems as such. Women are not usually war poets. They are not primary agents of conflict; they do not sign or violate treaties. They are rarely at the front line.

Nevertheless, their perceptions of the aftermath of war may be especially keen. Just as the soldier at the front may write the most engaged war poems, so women, always a less powerful unit of society, may document the lurch from great power to its loss—something that Germany suffered in just a few decades—in a particularly acute way.

And so the women poets in this book seem to shift the entire category of war poetry into after-war poetry. That they also seem to write here with remarkably similar tones and themes should be no surprise. As Lisel Mueller says in her superb book of translations of Marie Luise Kaschnitz, "There was no way for these writers and those of the next generation to write except in the context of that catastrophe and the evil which led to it."

In fact these are rarely poems of public reference. I have deliberately chosen poems that display the broadest vocabulary of loss—a breadth that seems to me in keeping with the richness and surprise of this work. The private vulnerability—the crashing in of a beloved world of almost secret perceptions—is often the deepest truth of historical tragedy.

Therefore I have been drawn to the detail of Nelly Sachs's amethyst, its old lights a sudden sign for new death. To the wonderful railways in Rose Ausländer's poem "Strangers," signaling the endless, stateless displacement of people shuffling those platforms without a destination. To the big gray birds in Bachmann's poem about leaving England. These fragments, rags, torn pieces of perception are sometimes healed here into wonderful poems, and sometimes not. But their power is unquestionable.

In these poems, also, are some of the most violated domestic interiors I know of in all poetry: Else-Lasker Schüler's gray flowers and her blue piano, in the shadow of the cellar door. Hilde Domin's dreamlike waterlogged doors in the city of Cologne. Rose Ausländer's eerie still life of a table with wine and bread and strawberries in the shadow of the ghetto. Nelly Sachs's carpet burnt by the fiery feet of a stateless person.

The political poem is an elusive category. The absolute privacy and reticence of some of these poems may not at first seem to fit that category. Yet in many instances, these poems show how the privacies and sidelinings of a woman's life—the silences of mothers and daughters, the individual life swept away by remote decisions, the shattered existence of families—affect a poetic perspective in a time of catastrophic violence. It is the very powerlessness of these lost entities which becomes, with hindsight, both a retrieval system and a searing critique of power. In that sense, of course, these are defining political poems.

## IV

I am profoundly interested in that bleak landscape which follows war or—in the minds of certain writers here—anticipates it. If I understand it rightly, that terrain is an extraordinary and reliable sign of dispossession, sometimes the only reference left of a land which once existed, full of human hope and ordinariness.

My interest is not abstract. During the Troubles in Ireland the political life of the island was endlessly on view—violent, oppressive, and often cruel. Gradually, act by murderous act, a country I had once known, once understood to have existed, disappeared. With that disappearance, a world of familiar signs—of memories and explanations—was displaced.

What's more, as that land disappeared there was little enough to register its previous existence. The delicacy and actuality of a place in its time can quickly be overwritten.

But the political poem in Ireland did register that disappearing country. Visibly, eloquently, that poem became a fever chart of the events around it. As it did so, something striking happened. The more it registered the political upheaval the less it became a public poem. The less it became a public poem, the more available it was to the private world which is the site of the deepest injury in a time of violence.

The truth was, that the violation of our island went so deep, was so toxic, that the private could no longer find shelter from the public. Everything was touched. Nothing was spared: A buckled shoe in a market street after a bombing. A woman looking out a window at an altered street—they were all emblems, images, perhaps even graffiti of the new reality. Overnight, so it seemed, the division between the public and private imagination ceased to be meaningful. Both were interchangeable ways of grasping and rendering a new reality. The political poem became a map of dissolving boundaries.

I do not mean to compare what happened on one island to the mid-century cataclysm which these poets knew and endured. Nevertheless, I do believe my experience of the first made me more able to read these beautiful poems for what they are—one of the most poignant acoustic systems of all: the vast public event felt as a private tremor.


## V

From the Baltic and North seas to the north German plain, from the Harz mountains to the dry, sharp air of the Alps, Germany defines itself through differences. *Deutschland? aber wo liegt es?* (Germany? but where is it?) was the question raised by Goethe and Schiller. Throughout the nineteenth century, Germany was assigned the mainland European virtues of intellectual grandeur, scholarly persistence, and a profoundly Romantic self-perception of its own history and culture.

The real country has its own commanding scholars and historians. I am concerned here with something else. That is, with the country which many of these poems suggest: an invisible terrain which consists in what was lost even more than in what was ruined. A virtual geography unfolds here in the poignant, often heartbroken acts of remembrance and outrage.

It is important to remember the source of that outrage. Many of the women here were exiles; most, although not all, were Jewish.

This fact is central. An overwhelming historic tragedy marks this work and drives these poems toward a unique intersection between public and private expression. It also signals their involvement—as citizens, as artists, as helpless human beings—in a terrible communal event from which no one was privately exempt. These poems seek no shelter; these poets found none. Their authors are witnesses and participants both—a stance which is shared between all the poets in this book.

Some of the poems here come from the late 1930s; a few from as late as the 1980s. The majority are from the years in between. In every case however, the retrospect is of a series of events and losses which occurred around the war. Sometimes these were written up late—Ausländer's first postwar volume, *Blinder Sommer*, for instance, was not published until 1965.

In any case, there is no attempt here at an official or exact chronology. What matters is that the invisible land, the ghostly terrain which finally falls out of sight of historians and may be forgotten across generations, and yet shapes more of our inward world even now than we may realize, is rendered here with stunning force and consistency.

In this sense, these poets are mapmakers. Their poems reconstruct the elements of a shattered world. Homelessness, exile, and dispossession may well be the chief themes here. This is not just a new Europe, although it is certainly that. It is also a premonitory wasteland.

# VI

The years turn into decades. Each generation overwrites the previous one. By and large we have forgotten—it has faded—that iconography of station platforms, monochrome skies, borders, papers, ration books, refugees, broken cities, and skylines defined by rubble which the aftermath of a great war brings. We can still look at the photographs. We can still access those legends of horror from the histories of the time. Yet the poems in this book allow us to experience the local and its sibling aspect, the universal, in ways no temporal document could ever manage.

It seems to me that this is the angle at which these poems detach from their country, and even from their language. That what they suggest is not simply an outcome of German history, or of the war, or even of European history. It is more than that. These poems re-create that moment when poetry itself is called into question, when language is tested almost beyond its limits, when a vocabulary comes to the edges of the poem which the poem can hardly bear.

There is a progression here. The poems near the start of this book, nearest that is to the chronology of conflict, are steeped in the recoil. As time goes on it is the interior exile, the disaffections of language and memory which become the dominant theme. As I read these poems, what strikes me most is the gradual, radical probing of the actual constructs of where we live, the exploration of whether place, nation, home—*heimat* itself—is a fiction. When that fiction is swept away by cataclysm, then what is left? Often, according to these poems, it is just the words that describe the loss. Ausländer's wonderful lines, *Ich lebe / in meinem Mutterland—/ Wort* (I live / in my Motherland—/the Word), stand for this.

And poem after poem echoes it. Sachs's traveler from far away holds his native land in his arms, an orphan for whom he is trying to find a grave. Else Lasker-Schüler's blue piano, that infinitely poignant emblem of loss and freedom, is out-of-use, lost to music, a neighborhood for rats. Bachmann's beheaded angel is trying to bury hatred. Dagmar Nick's no-man's-land is a place of neither here nor there, a zone where touch and understanding have broken down.

It may seem wayward to argue that an unhistorical reading of these poems, steeped as they are in what happened and when, may be the deepest reading of all. And yet it may be.

## VII

There is always a starting point, a place where a project begins to turn into a passion. For me it was Elisabeth Langgässer's poem *Frühling 1946*. There is just one fractured, unlineated prose version of this poem in a single English-language anthology. It does not otherwise—and I have certainly searched far and wide for it—exist in a poetic translation in English. Once again to the best of my knowledge, it never has.

I am baffled by this. The poem is both bittersweet and radically revealing of its moment. It was written for Langgässer's daughter, Cordelia, on her release from Auschwitz-Birkenau after two years there, when she was sixteen. Langgässer had barely escaped deportation herself.

The poem is unrhetorical and obstinately lyrical, determined on renewal but with dark tones of an inconsolable sense of waste. It speaks of the "toad's domain" and of the Gorgon. It addresses the recovered child as "Holde Anemone" (sweet Anemone). It packs into closely structured stanzas, into myth, legend, and music, one aspect of an almost untellable story.

While I was working with it I happened on Cordelia Edvardson's memoir *Burned Child Seeks the Fire*. She is, of course, the daughter of the poem. She was also, as a child, assigned to assist Josef Mengele in Auschwitz-Birkenau.

The angle made between the poem and the memoir is compelling and wrenching. The connections go deep. The decorum of the poem is a disguise for the chaos of grief. While conversely the chaotic narrative of the memoir discloses a daughter's decorous love for a mother. I understand that in many ways such suffering remains inscrutable. What I understand far less is why this poem—

this essential song from a circle of the underworld—did not make its way safely from one language to another.

## VIII

Most translators have mixed motives and debts of honor, and mine in both cases are more than most. The motives first.

It is now thirty years since a Dutch journalist came to Dublin. She was making a radio program about Irish poets. She interviewed me in the quiet suburb in which I lived, a few miles from the city center. Ireland was just at the start of its ordeal. Reports came in almost daily of neighborhood violence in the North. Meanwhile, Irish poetry looked back to its old roots and heroic influences. No one yet knew how the two would engage in a grim dance of meaning and reference over the next two decades.

It is she who first spoke to me about Ingeborg Bachmann, one of the poets in this book. Bachmann had recently died in a tragic fire in Rome. The journalist spoke with feeling of her power, her reach, her confrontation of the postwar reality of Germany.

Bachmann was still a young woman when peace came to Germany. Her poems are filled with references to a land of uncertainty and shaken truths. Again, to use the Irish example, the peace which follows conflict is essential and welcome. But the aftermath can often put a strange, coarse varnish on events. The winners want to invent; the people want to forget. And that matrix, to the skeptical eye, can often look like the source-waters of history. But there is always a different place. A place where the unfinished business of broken truths and toxic words is carried forward. Art is one of those places. Bachmann practiced that art.

Over the years I came to know Bachmann's poetry. Its bleak strength was one of my reference points, something at the back of my mind. I could say that Bachmann's work is one of the motives for these translations and it would be a partial truth, but only partial.

One of my chief motives here has been simply to arrange this work so that the reader can follow it. Follow it, that is, off the pages of this book into other books. Into the mystery and adventure of how a poet confronts time with language. And also into the details of how the confrontation occurred. For that reason I have included notes at the back of this volume to explain circumstances or locations or events whenever I have felt such explanations would add to the reader's sense of the work. I have also included checklists—less complete than I would like—for further reading.

My sense of a reader discovering some of these wonderful poems for the first time—although there are many who already know them—dictated my practical choices as a translator. Although I have often felt diffident about doing this book, knowing there are other translators, let alone other poets, who can do this better. I have persisted simply because there are poets and poems here that are not well known in English and that deserve to be.

For this and other reasons, I decided early on that I would be as faithful as possible to the original text. While recognizing the difference between what a poem says and what it means—and the effects of this in another language—it seemed most important to represent these poems and poets as faithfully and accurately as possible. Although there is a long, rich and distinguished improvisational tradition in translation, I have not attempted to add any thing to it, even if I could. I wanted these translations to be windows, not veils. Where I have departed from this it has been after a lot of thought, and with real reluctance.

## IX

My debts are many. I was radically encouraged at every turn by the translations and commentaries by other scholars and poets who worked in this field. Sometimes these poems were hard to find. Sometimes these poets appeared unknown to a great many people.

Slowly, and with difficulty, I found what I needed. Only by searching on-line, by hunting through catalogs, could I get some of the early books.

Often I have waited eagerly for the mail to bring the one paperback—perhaps the small turquoise and coral copy of Ausländer's selected poems, translated by Ewald Osers—which would open another door into that poet's work. The wait was always worth it. These fine and essential poets have had some of the most eloquent advocates, and careful translators, any poets could wish for. In some cases it makes it more of a puzzle that many of these poets are not more widely read in English.

Although it may be cumbersome to name them, these books and scholars have been such companions that I should. Lisel Mueller, for her splendid translations of Kaschnitz. *Dark Soliloquy*, with Henry A. Smith's fine translations of Gertrud Kolmar and the illuminating foreword by Cynthia Ozick. Peter Filkins's groundbreaking book on Bachmann, *Songs in Flight*, with its foreword by Charles Simic. Jim Barnes's truly exemplary translations of Dagmar Nick. The immensely valuable English language versions of Else Lasker-Schüler by Janine Canan, Audri Durchslat-Litt, and Jeanette Litman-Demeestre. And, always, the pioneering work of Michael Hamburger and Christopher Middleton which made visible so much German poetry in English, as well as the fine work of Reinhold Grimm and Irmgard Elsner Hunt.

I am grateful to Nick Jenkins, my friend and colleague and the series editor here, and himself a fine scholar of poetry, for the early conversations—and the later ones—which helped me anchor this project in my own mind. To Ellen Foos for her scrupulous copyediting of the text. To Mary Murrell at Princeton, for her courtesy and enthusiasm. To John Felstiner, also a friend and colleague, to whom I spoke of the project, and whose own work on Paul Celan must always be a radiant inspiration to anyone who turns in this direction. To Dr. Regina Casper at Stanford, for her eloquent conversation one evening which gave me a vivid sense of the stature of Else Lasker-Schüler. To Dagmar Logie, also a friend, in the English Department who, at a very busy moment, cast her keen eye on some lines of poetry for me.

But my most particular thanks are due to Alys Xavier George, a doctoral student at Stanford. She came late into this project, when I had translated the poems and had lived with them enough to have a keen and anxious sense of my limitations. By that time I inhabited a strange translator's realm of shadows: I could feel the poems on the page, could remember the sound of words, could catch the music of the movement. But I knew I could not be certain of idioms—to mention only a few of my misgivings—and could never have an exact sense of the time zones the German language stows away into its verbs.

I hoped therefore Alys might catch my mistakes. She did far, far more than that. While hardly ever suggesting an alternative, she further opened the world of these poems to me by being what any translator can only dimly hope for: the conscience of the original poem. Her extraordinary perception of the meaning of a line or a phrase—itself her tribute to the integrity of these poems in their time and in their language—allowed me a still deeper involvement with them. There were times when my English simply did not collect and ferry safely over that integrity. That was my fault, not hers. This book has given me many rewards, and my conversations with her, across two languages but with a single view of the power and importance of these poems, is certainly one of them.

I owe special thanks to my husband, Kevin Casey, for his support and enthusiasm. He was my first reader. And to Jody Allen-Randolph, who listened with patience and respect as the project evolved.

In addition, my thanks are due to Elizabeth Bernhardt of the German Department at Stanford who introduced me to Alys.

Finally, the largest debt is to these poets. Reading their work, and writing their work, has provided me with a privileged view of the resilience of language, music, and resolution in the hardest of times. These are poems about darkness; they are not dark poems. In fact, they are documents of the human spirit. As such, they cannot be spared—in any language.

Eavan Boland
*Stanford and Dublin, 2003*

# Rose Ausländer

1901–1988

# A BIOGRAPHICAL NOTE

*Rose Ausländer* was born Rosalie Scherzer into a traditional Jewish family in Czernowitz in May 1901. She thus became a native of one of the most volatile boundaries of the old Austria. She was the elder of two children. Her father, Sigmund Scherzer, was a rabbinical student. She learned both Yiddish and Hebrew at home.

She attended the University of Czernowitz where her interest in philosophy began. In 1920, following the death of her father, as well as the passing of Bukovina to Romanian administration, she emigrated to the United States with fellow student, Ignaz Ausländer. They were married in 1923. They separated in 1926.

In 1931 after her divorce was finalized she returned to her home in Czernowitz to look after her invalid mother. She worked as a teacher and pursued an active literary life. Her first book of poems, *Der Regenbogen* (The Rainbow) was published in 1939 in a small edition of 400. It was widely praised in Bukovina but, because of her Jewish identity, had no currency in Nazi Germany.

She returned to New York in 1939 but after a few months, anxious to be reunited with her family, she went back to Czernowitz. In 1941 Czernowitz was occupied by Nazi troops and the ghetto was closed. She remained there for three years, often sheltering in cellars. While there, she met Paul Celan. Of this time she said "while we waited for death, there were those of us who dwelt in dreamwords—our traumatic home amidst our homelessness. To write was to live."

She moved back to New York in 1946 and published her poems there in both English and German. Her first post-war book was *Blinder Sommer* (Blind Summer) published in Vienna in 1965; *Ohne Visum* (Without Papers) was published in 1974; *Andere Zeichen* (Other Signs) came out in 1975.

By the mid-sixties she had decided to return to Germany. The last two decades of her life were spent in the Nelly Sachs Home for the Jewish Elderly in Düsseldorf. She received many prizes and honors in her later years. She died in Düsseldorf in 1988. Ausländer's poems are revelatory: lyric, questing, elegiac, and direct. They chronicle an extraordinary journey through languages, homelands, memories, and recoveries. At a profound level she understood that both language and identity had been uniquely tempered in her lifetime and by her experience. Her poems are the measure of that experience.

## Mutterland

Mein Vaterland ist tot
sie haben es begraben
im Feuer

Ich lebe
in meinem Mutterland—
Wort

## Motherland

My Fatherland is dead.
They buried it
in fire

I live
in my Motherland—
Word

*Damit kein Licht uns liebe*

Sie kamen
mit scharfen Fahnen und Pistolen
schossen alle sterne und den Mond ab
Damit kein Licht uns bliebe
Damit kein Licht uns liebe

Da begruben wir die Sonne
Es war eine unendliche Sonnenfinsternis

# So That No Light Would Be There to Love Us

And so they came
with shrill flags and guns.
They shot down all the stars. They shot down the moon
so that no light would be there above us
so that no light would be there to love us.

And then we buried the sun—
it was an endless eclipse of the sun

## Am Ende der Zeit

Wenn der Krieg beendet ist
am Ende der Zeit

gehn wir wieder spazieren
in der Muschelallee
einverstanden
mit Mensch und Mensch

Es wird schön sein
wenn es sein wird

am Ende der Zeit

## At the End of Time

When the war is over
when time has come to an end

we'll walk again
down an alley of mussel shells
and feel our oneness
with this man
and that man.

It will be wonderful
if and when that happens

when time has come to an end.

## Verwundert

Wenn der Tisch nach Brot duftet
Erdbeeren der Wein Kristall

denk an den Raum aus Rauch
Rauch ohne Gestalt

Noch nicht abgestreift
das Ghettokleid

sitzen wir um den duftenden Tisch
verwundert
dass wir hier sitzen

## Amazed

When the table is fragrant with bread
strawberries and with crystal wine

turn your mind to the chamber of smoke—
that smoke without a shape—

the garments of the ghetto
not yet stripped away—

and we sit around the fragrant table
amazed that we are sitting here.

## Die Fremden

Eisenbahnen bringen die Fremden
die aussteigen und sich ratlos umsehn.
In ihren Augen schwimmen
ängstliche Fische.
Sie tragen fremde Nasen
traurige Lippen.

Niemand holt sie ab.
Sie warten auf die Dämmerung
die kiene Unsterschiede macht
dann dürfen sie ihre Verwandten besuchen
in der Milchstrasse
in den Mulden des Monds.

Einer spielt Mundharmonika—
seltsame Melodien.
Eine andre Tonleiter wohnt
im Instrument:
eine unabhörbare Folge von
Einsamkeiten.

## Strangers

Railways bring strangers.
They disembark and look around:
they are helpless. Anxious fish
swim in their eyes.
They wear strange noses.
They have sad lips.

No one has come to fetch them.
They wait for the twilight
which makes no distinctions between them
so they can call on their kindred
in the Milky Way,
in the lunar hollows.

One plays a harmonica—
off-kilter melodies.
Another musical scale
lives inside the instrument:
an inaudible sequencing
of isolations.

## Meine Nachtigall

Meine Mutter war einmal ein Reh.
Die goldbraunen Augen
die Anmut
blieben ihr aus der Rehzeit.

Hier war sie
halb Engel halb Mensch—
die Mitte war Mutter.
Als ich sie fragte was sie gern geworden wäre
sagte sie: eine Nachtigall.

Jetzt ist sie eine Nachtigall.
Nacht um Nacht höre ich sie
im Garten meines schlaflosen Traumes.
Sie singt das Zion der Ahnen
sie singt das alte Österreich
sie singt die Berge und Buchenwälder
der Bukowina.
Wiegenlieder
singt mir Nacht um Nacht
meine Nachtigall
im Garten meines schlaflosen Traumes.

## My Nightingale

My mother was a doe in another time.
Her honey-brown eyes
and her loveliness
survive from that moment.

Here she was—
half an angel and half humankind—
the center was *mother*.
When I asked her once what she would have wanted to be
she made this answer to me: a nightingale.

Now she is a nightingale.
Every night, night after night, I hear her
in the garden of my sleepless dream.
She is singing the Zion of her ancestors.
She is singing the long-ago Austria.
She is singing the hills and beech-woods
of Bukowina.
My nightingale
sings lullabies to me
night after night
in the garden of my sleepless dream.

## Im Chagall-Dorf

Schiefe Giebel
hängen am
Horizont.

Der Brunnen schlummert
beleuchtet von
Katzenaugen.

Die Bäuerin
melkt die Ziege
im Traumstall.

Blau
der Kirschbaum am Dach
wo der bärtige Greis
geigt.

Die Braut
schaut ins Blaumenaug
schwebt auf dem Schleier
über der Nachtsteppe.

Im Chagall-Dorf
weidet die Kuh
auf der Mondweise
goldne Wölfe
beschützen die Lämmer.

## In Chagall's Village

The horizon
is hung
with crooked gables.

The well slumbers,
lit by
the eyes of cats.

In the dream-stable
the farmer's wife
is milking the goat.

The cherry tree up on the roof
is blue
and the old man with the beard
is playing the violin.

The bride
floats on her veil
over the Night-Steppe,
gazes into the eye of a flower.

In Chagall's village
the cow is grazing
in the moon-meadow.
Gilded wolves
keep watch over the lambs.

## Biographische Notiz

Ich rede
von der brennenden Nacht
die gelöscht hat
der Pruth

von Trauerweiden
Blutbuchen
verstummtem Nachtigallsang

vom gelben Stern
auf dem wir
stündlich starben
in der Galgenzeit

nicht über Rosen
red ich

Fliegend
auf einer Luftschaukel
Europa Amerika Europa

ich wohne nicht
ich lebe

## Biographical Note

I speak
of the burning night
extinguished by
the Pruth.

Of weeping willows,
copper beeches.
Of the nightingale's song falling silent.

Of the yellow star
on which we died
hour by hour
in the age of the Hangman.

I do not speak
about roses

flying on a swingboat
Europe America Europe.

I do not reside.
I live.

## Mein Schlüssel

Mein Schlüssel
hat das Haus verloren

Ich gehe von Haus zu Haus
keines paßt

Den Schlosser
habe ich gefunden

mein Schlüssel paßt
zu seinem Grab

## My Key

My key
has lost its house.

I go from house to house
but none fits.

I have found
the locksmith.

My key fits
into his grave.

# Elisabeth Langgässer

1899–1950

# A BIOGRAPHICAL NOTE

*Elisabeth Langgässer* was born in 1899 in the market town of Alzey in southwestern Germany. Her mother was Christian. She herself was raised Catholic. Her architect father, Eduard Langgässer, was Jewish.

Langgässer went to the Höhere Mädchenschule in Alzey. She qualified as a teacher and between 1921–24 taught elementary school in Griesheim and Darmstadt. By this time, she was already writing. Her first volume of poems *Der Wendekreis des Lammes* (The Turning Circle of the Lambs) was published in 1924.

In Griesheim she met Hermann Heller, also of Jewish origin, by whom she had a daughter Cordelia in 1929. That year she moved to Berlin with her mother and grandmother. There, she was drawn to the writers around the magazine *Kolonne*. She came to know such poets as Günter Eich and Peter Huchel. She was particularly influenced by the nature poet Wilhelm Lehmann.

In 1933 she published *Proserpina*. In the same year, she met and married Willhelm Hoffmann, who was non-Jewish. Their marriage was unsanctioned since, in 1935, the anti-Jewish Nuremberg Laws forbade any inter-racial marriage. In the same year, she was prohibited from writing by the Nazi Reich Literature Chamber. This amounted to a professional disqualification, cutting her off from income as well as publication.

In 1941, her daughter Cordelia was required to wear the yellow star. Langgässer made frantic efforts to save her daughter, even managing to get her a Spanish passport. Despite this, in 1944 Cordelia was deported first to Theresienstadt, then to Auschwitz-Birkenau. A year later, Elisabeth Langgässer was diagnosed with multiple sclerosis.

Elisabeth Langgässer wrote both poetry and prose. After the war she published *Der Torso* (The Torso), 1947 and *Das Labyrinth* (The Labyrinth), 1949. Her novel *Das unauslöschliche Siegel* (The Indelible Seal) was widely read after the war. In 1950 she published *Märkische Argonautenfahrt*. Her books of poetry are as follows: *Der Wendekreis des Lammes* (The Turning Circle of the Lambs), 1924, *Die Tierkreisgedichte* (The Animal Circle Poems), 1935. *Der Laubmann und die Rose* (The Leaf Man and the Rose), 1947. Her poetry, in particular, is almost impossible to find in English. One novel, *The Quest*, was published in the United States in 1953. Her work—philosophic, Christian, formal, mythological—fell somewhat out of fashion in the modernist postwar era.

Her themes were those of the Christian nature poem—a lyric of grace and renewal. That theme is powerfully tested here in *Frühling 1946*, written on the release of her daughter Cordelia from Auschwitz. Langässer's poem opens an extraordinary window into the undocumented, harrowing reunions after the war, when survivors from the camps rejoined their loved ones. Langässer died in Karlsruhe, in 1950, of complications brought about by multiple sclerosis.

## Frühling 1946

Holde Anemone,
Bist du wieder da
Und erscheinst mit heller Krone
Mir Gerschundenem zum Lohne
Wie Nausikaa?

Windbewegtes Bücken,
Woge, Schaum und Licht!
Ach, welch sphärisches Entzücken
Nahm dem staubgebeugten Rücken
Endlich sein Gewicht?

Aus dem Reich der Kröte
Steige ich empor,
Unterm Lid noch Plutons Röte
Und des Totenführers Flöte
Gräßlich noch im Ohr.

Sah in Gorgos Auge
Eisenharten Glanz,
Ausgesprühte Lügenlauge
Hört' ich flüstern, daß sie tauge
Mich zu töten ganz.

Anemone! Küssen
Laß mich dein Gesicht:
Ungespiegelt von den Flüssen
Styx und Lethe, ohne Wissen
Um das Nein und Nicht.

## Spring 1946

So you return
My sweet Anemone—
All brilliant stamen, calyx, crown—
Making it worth the devastation,
Like Nausicaa?

Windblown and bowing—
Wave and spray and light—
What whirling joy at last
Has lifted up this weight
From shoulders bent with dust?

Now I arise
Out of the toad's domain—
Pluto's reddish glare still under my eyelids—
And the hideous pipe of the guide to the dead
Still in my ears.

I have seen the iron gleam
In the Gorgon's eye.
I have heard the hiss, the whisper,
The rumor that she would kill me:
It was a lie.

Anemone, my daughter,
Let me kiss your face: it is
Unmirrored by the waters
Of Lethe or of Styx.
And innocent of *no* or *not*.

Ohne zu verführen
Lebst und bist du da,
Still mein Herz zu rühren,
Ohne es zu schüren—
Kind Nausikaa!

And see, you are alive
And here—there's no deception—
And quiet in the way you touch my heart
Yet do not rake its fires—
My child, my Nausicaa!

# Nelly Sachs

1891–1970

# A BIOGRAPHICAL NOTE

*Nelly (Leonie) Sachs* was born in 1891 into a comfortable Jewish home in the fashionable Tiergarten suburb of Berlin. As the only child of a prosperous inventor and entrepreneur, William Sachs (her mother was Margareta Karger Sachs), she was privately educated, learning music, dance, and painting. She then entered the Berliner Höhere Töchterschule.

As a young girl of fifteen she began a correspondence with Selma Lagerlöf, the Swedish writer, a connection that would prove crucial to her survival when the war years began in Germany.

Sachs continued to live in Berlin with her mother after the death of her father in 1930. But as the Nazi grip tightened in the city and Jews became more vulnerable to the new laws of exclusion and persecution, she and her mother determined to escape. Through the intervention of Selma Lagerlöf, Sachs and her mother were granted asylum in Sweden in 1940. There they lived in a two-bedroom apartment while Nelly Sachs made a modest living translating Swedish poets into German.

During this time she also worked on new poems which were first seen in the volume *In den Wohnungen des Todes* (In the Habitations of Death) which was published in Berlin in 1947. It contained a sequence of elegies that confirmed her transformation as a writer. It was effectively her first book of poems. Elements of Hasidic mysticism were crafted together with German Romanticism and echoes of the Psalms into signature elegies. Describing her own project Nelly Sachs said it was "in this night of nights to give some idea of the holy darkness."

After the war, and following the death of her mother in 1950, she remained in Stockholm. Although she had several break-downs, she continued to write and publish. Among her many published books were: *Sternverdunkelung* (Eclipse of the Stars), 1949; *Eli: Ein Mysterienspiel vom Leiden Israels* (Eli: A Mystery Play of the Sufferings of Israel), 1951; *Und Neimand Weiss Weiter* (And No One Knows How to Go On), 1957; and *Flucht und Verwandlung* (Flight and Metamorphosis), 1959. In 1966, she won the Nobel Prize in Literature and her citation praised her for "lyrical laments of painful beauty and . . . dramatic legends." She died of cancer in 1970.

Nelly Sachs's poetry has been described as belonging to "the great laments of literature." *In den Wohnungen des Todes* was acclaimed as a document of grief, outrage, and renewal. Poems such as "O, der weinenden Kinder Nacht!" (O, the Night of the Weeping Children!) provided compelling proof that the terrible events of the Holocaust were not, after all, unimaginable.

## Wenn ich nur wüsste

Wenn ich nur wüsste
Worauf dein letzter Blick ruhte.
War es ein Stein, der schon veile letzte Blicke
Getrunken hatte, bis sie in Blindheit
Auf den Blinden fielen?

Oder war es Erde
Genug, um einen Schuh zu füllen,
Und schon schwarz geworden
Von soviel Abscheid
Und von soviel Tod bereiten?

Oder war es dein letzer Weg,
Der dir das Lebewohl von allen Wegen brachte
Die du gegangen warst?

Eine Wasserlache, ein Stück spiegelndes Metall,
Vielleicht die Gürtelschnalle deines Feindes,
Oder irgend ein anderer, kleiner Wahrsager
Des Himmels?

Oder sandte die diese Erde,
Die kienen ungeliebt von hinnen gehen lässt
Ein Vogelzeichen durch die Luft,
Erinnernd deine Seele, dass sie zuckte
In ihrem qualverbrannten Leib?

## If I Only Knew

If I only knew
where you put that last look.
Was it on a stone,
a blind stone,
which had taken in so many last looks
that they fell blindly on its blindness?

Or was it on a shoeful of earth?
Already black
with so many partings,
so many killings?

Or was it on your last road
saying farewell to you from all the other roads
you once walked?

A puddle? A glitter of metal?
The buckle of your enemy?
Some other spirit-augury
of the world to come?

Or did this earth which lets
no one depart without its love
send you the sign
of a bird in the air,
reminding your soul
that it flinched just so
in its charred and tortured body?

## In der blauen Ferne

In der blauen Ferne
wo die rote Apfelbaumallee wandert
mit himmelbesteigenden Wurzelfüßen
wird die Sehnsucht destilliert
für Alle, die im Tale leben.

Die Sonne, am Wegesrand liegend
mit Zauberstäben
gebietet Halt den Reisenden.

Die bleiben stehn
im gläsernen Albtraum
während die Grille fein kratzt
am Unsichtbaren

und der Stein seinen Staub
tanzend in Muzik verwandelt.

## In the Blue Distance

For all those who live in the valley
yearning is distilled
in the blue distance
with its straggling red row of apple trees—
rooted feet climbing the skyline.

The sun,
lying in wait by the roadside
with magic wands,
commands travelers to come to a halt.

They stand still in this bad dream
with its glazed surfaces,
while the cricket scratches daintily
at what-cannot-be-seen

and the dancing stone
transforms its dust into music.

## Bereit sind alle Länder aufzustehn

Bereit sind alle Länder aufzustehn
vond der Landkarte.
Abzuschütteln ihre Sternenhaut
die blauen Bündel ihrer Meere
auf dem Rücken zu knüpfen
ihre Berge mit den Feuerwurzeln
als Mützen auf die rauchenden Haare zu setzen.

Bereit das letze Schwermutgewicht
im Koffer zu tragen, diese Schmetterlingspuppe,
auf deren Flügeln sie die Riese einmal
beenden werden.

## All the Lands of the Earth

All the lands of the earth
are ready
to rise up off the surface of the map
to shrug off their epidermis of stars
to tie the cerulean bundles of ocean
on their back
to set the mountains with their deep roots of fire
as caps on top of their smoking hair.

They are ready to carry that last
deadweight of sadness with them as baggage:
as a chrysalis on whose wings
one day
they will end the journey.

## In der Flucht

In der Flucht
welch großer Empfang
unterwegs—

Eingehüllt
in der Winde Tuch
Füße im Gebet des Sandes
der niemals Amen sagen kann
denn er muß
von der Flosse in den Flügel
und weiter—

Der kranke Schmetterling
weiß bald wieder vom Meer—
Dieser Stein
mit der Inschrift der Fliege
hat sich mir in die Hand gegeben—

An Stelle von Heimat
halte ich die Verwandlungen der Welt—

## In Flight

In flight—
and what a great reception
on the way—

Shawled
by the wind,
feet in the sand's prayer
who can never—
driven from fin to wing
and further—
say *amen*—

soon the ailing butterfly
will know about the ocean—
This stone
with the fly's inscription
gave itself into my hand

I hold,
instead of a homeland,
the transformations of the world.

## In diesem Amethyst

In diesem Amethyst
zind die Zeitalter der Nacht gelagert
und eine frühe Lichtintelligenz
zündete die Schwermut an
die war noch flüssig
und weinte

Immer noch glänzt dein Sterben
hartes Veilchen

## In This Amethyst

Age-old nighttime is
stored in this amethyst.
An early intelligence of light
set fire to this sadness
which then still flowed,
still wept.

And still your dying shines—
hard violet.

## Kommt einer von ferne

Kommt einer
von ferne
mit einer Sprache
die vielleicht die Laute
verschließt
mit dem Wiehern der Stute
oder
dem Piepen
junger Schwarzamseln
oder
auch wie eine knirschende Säge
die alle Nähe zerschneidet—

Kommt einer
von ferne
mit Bewegungen des Hundes
oder
vielleicht der Ratte
und es ist Winter
so kleide ihn warm
kann auch sein
er hat Feuer unter den Sohlen
(vielleicht ritt er
auf einem Meteor)
so schilt ihn nicht
falls dein Teppich durchlöchert schreit—

Ein Fremder hat immer
seine Heimat im Arm
wie eine Waise
für die er vielleicht nichts
als ein Grab sucht.

## If Someone Comes

If someone comes
from far away
speaking a language which
shuts itself up perhaps
in the whinnying of mares
or the chittering
of young blackbirds
or a screech-saw which shreds
everything near it—

If someone comes
from far away
who moves like a dog
or
maybe like a rat
and it is winter, then
put him in warm clothes—
he might have fire
at his footsoles
(maybe he rode in
on a meteor)
so don't scold him
if your carpet shrieks and is full of holes—

A stranger
always carries
his native land in his arms—
like an orphan
for which he might be seeking
nothing more nor less than a grave.

# Gertrud Kolmar

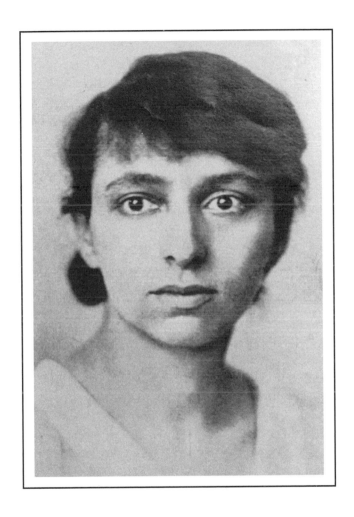

1894–1943

# A BIOGRAPHICAL NOTE

*Gertrud Kolmar's* life was cut off at the age of 48. She died in one of the Nazi death camps, almost certainly Auschwitz. Her poetry with its expansive, erotic, and original style was the product of an almost secret life of endeavor and commitment. Cynthia Ozick says of her: "The American poet she is most likely to remind us of is Emily Dickinson."

She was born Gertrud Chodziesner, the first child of Ludwig and Elise Chodziesner in December 1894. At the time of her birth, her father was a successful lawyer and the family lived in a comfortable suburb in Berlin.

She went to the local grammar school in Berlin, then the Höhere Mädchenschule Klockow, a private school for girls. At sixteen she left home and went to Leipzig to attend a home-economics school for girls. When she finished this she returned to Berlin and entered a teacher training school for interpreters where she learned French and English. She put these skills to good use when World War I broke out and was employed as an interpreter at the prisoner-of-war camp at Döberitz in Berlin.

Throughout World War I Gertrud Kolmar wrote steadily and accumulated a small body of poems. With the end of the war, her father decided to have them privately printed. A first volume of just seventy-two pages, called *Gedichte*, came out under the pen name Gertrud Kolmar in 1917.

In 1923 her family moved from Berlin to the rural area of Finkenkrug. She remained there for fifteen years, writing most of the work which formed her *Das Lyrishche Werk*, published long after her death. Her mother died in 1930 and she remained in Finkenkrug, looking after her father.

In 1938 her sister succeeded in getting out of Germany. She too planned to emigrate, but was detained by her obligations to an invalid father. In 1938 she saw the publication of her book *Die Frau und die Tiere* (The Woman and the Animals). But when *Kristallnacht* occurred that November, new laws were instituted. Jewish newspapers were closed down. Remaining copies of her book were destroyed. Gertrud Kolmar and her father were forced to sell their house under the new property laws.

In July 1941 she entered forced labor in a factory in Berlin-Lichtenberg. In 1942 she was moved to Charlottenburg. She maintained extraordinary fortitude. "I am a good match for today" she wrote. During these last few years of her life, she taught herself Hebrew and wrote poems in that language, though none have survived. In September 1942 her father was deported to Theresienstadt, where he died. Early in 1943 she was also deported. Her last letter is dated February 21, 1943. There is no trace of her after that.

## Das Opfer

Ihre purpurnen Schuhe kennen den Weg, und die Spange um
    ihren Knöchel weiß ihn.
So wandelt sie ohne Willen, gebunden, im Traum.
So wandeln die heißen dunkelnden Augen durch Reihen
    steinerner Flügelkatzen und schwerer bemalter Säulen
    zum Vorhof des Tempels,
Da ein nackter Greis in schmutzigem Lendentuche auf winziger
    Pauke hämmert und endlos sein näselnder Singsang
    fleht.
Die Aussätzige, von wirren Haaren verhangen, reckt stöhnend
    den Arm.
Unfruchtbare seufzen Gebete.
Em Jüngling steht hoch und steil, unbeweglich, mit breitem
    bronzenen Schwert,
Und ein Wahnsinniger krümmt mit leisem verzückten Lachen
    sich über rosengranitener Schwelle.
Wie sie vorüberstrebt, hascht die Kranke, Verdeckte nach ihrem
    Kleide, den amarantfarbenen Säumen;
Sie aber zieht, die Wolke, an unerreichbaren Abendhimmeln
    dahin.

Dreimal fragt ihre pochende Hand die kupferne Tür, die ihr
    dreimal erwidert.
Em Priester öffnet.
Sein Bart rinnt, blauer Fluß, über die linnene Bleiche des
    Untergewandes, den Safran des Mantels.
Auf seiner hohen schwarzen Haube spreizt ein silberner Vogel
    sich.
Er gießt Milch in rote Tonschalen, Milch der wachsweißen Kuh
    mit vergoldeten Hörnern,

## The Victim

Her shoes are purple: they know the way. Her ankle-bracelet
    knows the way as well.
She moves along, her will at bay: bound and in a dream.
Her eyes, hot and darkening, move past rows of stony, winged
    cats and thick, painted columns, and on into the
    forecourt of the temple where an old man, naked, in a
    filthy loincloth, beats a miniature kettledrum and wails
    an endless, high-pitched, nasal prayer.
A leper, with a face covered with tangled hair, reaches out an
    arm and groans.
Barren women sigh out their prayers.
A young man, tall and upright, stands there. He does not move.
    He holds a bronze sword with a broad blade.
On the rosy granite of the threshold, a lunatic twists in an ecstasy
    of laughter.
As she goes by, a sick woman, all covered up, snatches at her
    hem, with its colors of amaranth.
She drifts on. She is a cloud in the unreachable skies of the
    evening.


Three times her hand puts a question to the door. Three times it
    comes back with an answer.
A priest opens it.
His beard is a blue stream, flowing down over the bleached linen
    of his undergarment, his saffron yellow cloak.
A silver bird, with outspread wings, stands on his high black hat.
He pours milk into red clay vessels, the milk of the waxy white
    cow with gold horns—
This is the drink for the holy serpents

Trank den heiligen Schlangen,
Die ihre glatten, getuschten Leiber am Boden des düsternden
Raumes knäueln und wälzen.
Und eine großte chrysolithäugige hebt sich und lauscht und
wiegt den Bauch zu unhörbarem Liede.
Die Frau verneigt sich ihr, schirmt mit dem Finger das Auge
und küßt der Natter die Stirn. —
Sie schweigt
Und tritt hinaus in den leeren inneren Hof;
Nur perlmutterne Tauben picken Weizenkörner vom
lauchgrünen Nephrit.
Sie ängsten nicht.
Zwischen bunt beladenen Wänden hält streng und schmal eine
Ebenholzpforte sich,
Und dreimal rührt die Frau mit elfenbeinernem Stabe das
Schloß, das ihr Antwort weigert.
Sie bleibt und wartet.

Dort wird sie eingehn.
Unter dem Bilde des Abgotts mit goldenen Krötenschenkeln,
Im Rauche glimmenden Sandelholzes,
Beim Strahlen zuckenden Feuers
Wird der Fremde nahn,
Wird langsam schreiten und seine rechte Hand auf ihre Mitte
legen als ein Zeichen.
Er wird sie hinführen in den sengenden Kreis
Und ihre Brüste schauen
Und schweigend stark aus glühen Umarmungen Wollust
schmelzen.
Sie töten . . .
So ist es ihr vorbestimmt und sie weiß es.

Sie zaudert nicht. Kein Beben zwingt ihre Glieder; sie blickt
nicht um,

Who, as the light goes, writhe and knot their smooth, marked
  bodies on the hall floor.
A huge one, with eyes like chrysolite, rears up and listens and its
  belly sways to the unheard song.
The woman bows to it and covers her eyes with one finger and
  kisses the top of the adder's head.
She holds her tongue
And walks out into the empty inner courtyard.
Nothing there but mother-of-pearl pigeons pecking at grains of
  wheat on jade slabs, green as leeks.
They do not frighten her.
A narrow gate, a shape of stern ebony, stands between the richly
  colored walls.
The woman has an ivory wand. She strikes the lock three times.
  She is denied.
She stands and waits.


She will enter there
Under the image of the false god with his golden toad-like thighs
In the smoke from the glowing sandalwood
In the flicker of the firelight
The stranger will come
With a slow stride and will lay his hand as a sign on her midriff
And he will lead her into the burning circle
And will gaze at her breasts
And then silently, in his strength, he will melt lust from hot
  embraces
And will kill her . . .
It is her destiny. It has been decided. She knows it.


She does not hesitate. She does not tremble. She looks straight
  ahead.
She knows neither good fortune nor misfortune.

Kennt weder Glück noch Unglück.

Sie füllte sich ganz mit brennender Finsternis, mit dumpf
erglänzender Demut, die dem Gebote des Scheusals
dienen, dem goldenen Götzen sterben will. —

Doch in ihrem Herzen ist Gott.

Auf ihrem ernsten und schönen Antlitz haftet sein Siegel.

Das aber weiß sie nicht.

She filled herself entirely with the molten dark. With the ember
    light of humility that serves the commandment of the
    monster
and she will die for the golden idol—

Yet in her heart is God.
He has put his seal on her grave and lovely face.
But she does not know that.

# Else Lasker-Schüler

1869–1945

# A BIOGRAPHICAL NOTE

*Else Lasker-Schüler* was born, the youngest of six children, on February 11, 1869. "I was born in Thebes" she once wrote, referring to her love for fantastical identity "although I first saw the light in Elberfeld in the Rhineland." Her family was Jewish, but by this date largely assimilated. She was close to her mother. Her father, however, was a banker who had scant tolerance for daughters. "He did not appreciate girls very much" she wrote "and whenever I went out with him I had to be dressed in brazenly boyish clothes." This early distinctive culture of play and impersonation remained with her into adult life.

In 1894 she married Berthold Lasker, a physician. Five years later she had a son, Paul. In 1902 she published her first volume of poems, *Styx: Gedichte* (Styx: Poems) swiftly followed in 1905 by *Der Siebente Tag* (The Seventh Day).

In 1899 she divorced. She was remarried in 1904 to George Levin, one of the leaders of the Expressionist movement in Berlin. This marriage also failed. By now she was openly unconventional. In the early part of the century she was a central figure in the Berlin cafés which she described as "our nocturnal home . . . our oasis, our gypsy caravan." In 1909 she published a play *Die Wupper* (The Wupper) and an acclaimed volume of poems *Hebraische Balladen* (Hebrew Ballads) in 1913.

She traveled widely in the twenties, despite financial hardship. Her closest friends were Gottfried Benn and the painter Franz Marc. By these friendships, she allied herself with the freedom and experimentalism of Weimar Germany. Her own poetry was beginning to be rewarded at the start of the thirties—she won the prestigious Kleist Prize—but the Nazi movement was starting to encroach on and censor Expressionism. In 1933 a scuffle with Nazi brownshirts, in which she was beaten with an iron rod, made her flee to Zurich. The devastating event of these years was the death of her son Paul from tuberculosis in 1927. She never ceased to grieve his loss.

Lasker-Schüler's late years were displaced and lonely. She lived for the last six or so years in Jerusalem, in what was then Palestine. The outbreak of war prevented her return to Zurich. The displacement, the isolation, and an increasing imaginative acceptance of her fate is stated in her superb, visionary last book *Mein blaues Klavier* (My Blue Piano). It combines the playfulness and experimentation of her Expressionist roots with a profound, elegiac lyricism. She died in January 1945 of a heart attack and was buried on the Mount of Olives.

Yehudi Amichai, who used to see her when he was a boy, has written, "She is known around the world as one of the great poets of this century." And in 1953, at a poetry reading devoted to her work, Gottfried Benn called her "the greatest lyric poet Germany ever had." (*dies war die größte Lyrikerin, die Deutschland je hatte . . .*).

## Mein blaues Klavier

Ich habe zu Hause ein blaues Klavier
Und kenne doch keine Note.

Es steht im Dunkel der Kellertür,
Seitdem die Welt verrohte.

Es spielen Sternenhände vier
—Die Mondfrau sang im Boote—
Nun tanzen die Ratten im Geklirr.

Zerbrochen ist die Klaviatür. . . .
Ich beweine die blaue Tote.

Ach liebe Engel öffnet mir
—Ich aß vom bitteren Brote—
Mir lebend schon die Himmelstür—
Auch wider dem Verbote.

## My Blue Piano

At home I have a blue piano.
But I can't play a note.

It's been in the shadow of the cellar door
Ever since the world went rotten.

Four starry hands play harmonies.
The Woman in the Moon sang in her boat.
Now only rats dance to the clanks.

The keyboard is in bits.
I weep for what is blue. Is dead.

Sweet angels, I have eaten
Such bitter bread. Push open
The door of heaven. For me, for now —

Although I am still alive —
Although it is not allowed.

*Ich weiß*

Ich weiß, daß ich bald sterben muß
Es leuchten doch alle Bäume
Nach langersehntem Julikuß—

Fahl werden meine Träume—
Nie dichtete ich einen trüberen Schluß
In den Büchern meiner Reime.

Eine Blume brichst du mir zum Gruß—
Ich liebte sie schon im Keime.
Doch ich weiß, daß ich bald sterben muß.

Mein Odem schwebt über Gottes Fluß—
Ich setze leise meinen Fuß
Auf den Pfad zum ewigen Heime.

## I Know

Soon, I know, I must die
Since all the trees are shining
After the longed-for kiss of this July.

My dreams have faded out with time—
Never have I crafted such a dark conclusion
In my books of rhyme.

The flower you snap off to greet me
Is one I already loved when it was in the bud.
Soon, I know—despite it all—I must die.

My breath floats above God's river.
With a light step I set out
On the path for my eternal home.

# Herbst

Ich pflücke mir am Weg das letzte Tausendschön . . .
Es kam ein Engel mir mein Totenkleid zu nähen —
Denn ich muß andere Welten weiter tragen.

Das ewige Leben *dem*, der viel von Liebe weiß zu sagen.
Ein Mensch der *Liebe* kann nur auferstehen!
Haß schachtelt ein! wie hoch die Fackel auch mag
    schlagen.

Ich will dir viel viel Liebe sagen —
Wenn auch schon kühle Winde wehen,
In Wirbeln sich um Bäume drehen,
Um Herzen, die in ihren Wiegen lagen.

Mir ist auf Erden weh geschehen . . .
Der Mond gibt Antwort dir auf deine Fragen.
Er sah verhängt mich auch an Tagen,
Die zaghaft ich beging auf Zehen.

# Autumn

On my way, I pick the last daisy.
An angel has come to sew my shroud—
I must clothe myself in other worlds.

Eternal life to those who know enough
To talk a great deal about love.
Only those who love will rise again.
Hate is a prison, however high the torch burns above it.

I have so much, so much to say to you about love—
Even when the winds blow and are chill
And whirl around the trees
And round those hearts which once lay in their cradles.

I was injured on this earth.
Ask the moon—he will answer you.
Though overcast, he kept an eye on me
Even on those days I tiptoed through so timidly.

## Abends

Auf einmal mußte ich singen—
Und ich wußte nicht warum?
—Doch abends weinte ich bitterlich.

Es steig aus allen Dingen
Ein Schmerz, und der ging um
—Und legte sich auf mich.

## In the Evening

I had to do it—suddenly, I had to sing.
I had no idea why—
But when the evening came I wept. I wept bitterly.

Pain was everywhere. Sprang out of everything—
Spread everywhere. Into everything—
And then lay on top of me.

## Meine Mutter

Es brennt die Kerze auf meinen Tisch
Für meine Mutter die ganze Nacht—
Für meine Mutter. . . .

Mein Herz brennt unter dem Schulterblatt
Die ganze Nacht
Für meine Mutter. . . .

## My Mother

On my table the candle burns
All night for my mother—
For my mother. . . .

Under my shoulder blade my heart burns
All night
For my mother. . . .

## Über glitzernden Kies

Könnt ich nach Haus—
Die Lichte gehen aus—
Erlischt ihr letzter Gruß.

Wo soll ich hin?
Oh Mutter mein, weißt du's?
Auch unser Garten ist gestorben! . . .

Es liegt ein grauer Nelkenstrauß
Im Winkel wo im Elternhaus,
Er hatte große Sorgfalt sich erworben.

Umkräntze das Willkommen an den Toren
Und gab sich ganz in seiner Farbe aus.
Oh liebe Mutter! . . .

Versprühte Abendrot
Am Morgen weiche Sehnsucht aus
Bevor die Welt in Schmach und Not.

Ich habe keine Schwestern mehr und keine Brüder.
Der Winter spielte mit dem Tode in den Nestern
Und Reif erstarrte alle Liebeslieder.

## Over Glistening Gravel

At last, to go home —
The lights are going out—
Their final greeting is extinguished.

But where can I go?
My dear mother, do you even know?
Even our garden is dead . . .

In some lost corner of this family home
A bunch of grey-faced carnations
Was once tended with all our painstaking care.

Once it wreathed the door in its welcome
And wore out all its colors on us—
Oh my dear mother! . . .

And sprayed all around us a setting sun,
And in the morning time, such yearnings.
All this, before the world fell apart.

I have no brothers now. I have no sisters.
In every nest, winter has played with death.
A late frost has frozen out all the love songs.

## Ein einziger mensch

Ein einziger mensch ist oft ein ganzes Volk
Doch jeder eine Welt
Mit einem Himmelreich wenn
Er der Eigenschaften uredelste pflegt:
Gott.
Gott aufsprießen läßt in sich
Gott will nicht begossen sein mit Blut.
Wer seinen Nächtsten tötet
Tötet in ihm aufkeimend Gott.
Wir können nicht mehr schlafen in den Nächten
Und bangen mit den
Wir wollen.

## A Single Man

A single man can be a whole nation
Yet he becomes an earth
With its own heaven when
He nurtures the old and noble qualities:
God—
Lets God spring up in him—
God does not want to be watered in blood.
He who kills his own neighbor
Kills the God-seedling in his heart.
We cannot sleep at night.
We are afraid
For those we long for.

# Ingeborg Bachmann

1926–1973

# A BIOGRAPHICAL NOTE

*Ingeborg Bachmann* was born in Klagenfurt, Austria in 1926. She was twelve years old in 1938 when Hitler's troops marched into the main square. She marked the event as the end of her childhood. Later, she studied at the Universities of Graz and Innsbruck, did her graduate work on Martin Heidegger, and received a doctorate of philosophy in 1950.

In 1952 she read her poetry at a meeting of Gruppe 47, the newly formed and influential group of postwar German writers. The following year she published her first book of poems, *Die gestundete Zeit* (Borrowed Time) and received the Gruppe 47 prize. She continued to publish to acclaim and wide international interest. In 1956 she published her second volume of poems *Anrufung des großen Bären* (Invocation of the Great Bear). In 1959 she gave a noted series of lectures on poetics and philosophy at the University of Frankfurt.

By the end of the fifties, however, she had turned away, and with finality, from poetry. Although she published a handful more poems her output—never very large in any case—was thereafter almost exclusively in prose. Although her fiction, especially the later novel *Malina,* came to be critically esteemed, her abandonment of poetry troubled and confused her readers. All questions were left unanswered when she died in October 1973 in a tragic and mysterious fire in her apartment in Rome.

Despite the disruption of her early career, Ingeborg Bachmann must be counted as one of the most memorable voices to emerge in postwar writing. Hers is a voice that was not silenced by the shock and bleakness of war's aftermath, but instead recorded it unswervingly. She is remembered as a compelling, off-kilter laureate of a broken Europe.

Her achievement is the outcome of a unique intersection of land and language. Born in Carinthia, a southernmost province of Austria, bordered by the provinces of the Tirol on the northwest and east, Salzburg and Styria on the north, Slovenia on the southeast, and Italy on the southwest, her early poems show her to be a connoisseur of borders and border-languages.

In her celebrated lectures on poetics she stated: "we, who are preoccupied with language, have learned what speechlessness and muteness are—our, if you will, purest conditions!—and have returned from that no-man's-land with language which we will perpetuate as long as life is our own continuation." This struggle with meaning, this sense of its absolute peril and disruption following the war, was shared with older contemporaries like Paul Celan. But Bachmann was also of the new Germany—engaged with a different landscape of displacement. Charles Simic wrote, "Whoever in the future wishes to experience that all-pervading sense of exile our age has felt, should read Bachmann." Her poems are among the most compelling documents of what happened—and how it was felt and imagined—after the war.

## Alle Tage

Der Krieg wird nicht mehr erklärt,
sondern fortgesetzt. Das Unerhörte
ist alltäglich geworden. Der Held
bleibt den Kämpfen fern. Der Schwache
ist in die Feuerzonen gerückt.
Die Uniform des Tages ist die Geduld,
die Auszeichnung der armselige Stern
der Hoffnung über dem Herzen.

Er wird verliehen,
wenn nichts mehr geschieht,
wenn das Trommelfeuer verstummt,
wenn der Feind unsichtbar geworden ist
und der Schatten ewiger Rüstung
den Himmel bedeckt.

Er wird verliehen
für die Flucht von den Fahnen,
für die Tapferkeit vor dem Freund,
für den Verrat unwürdiger Geheimnisse
und die Nichtachtung
jeglichen Befehls.

## Every Day

War is no longer declared:
Just continued. The unheard-of
has become the quotidian.
The hero weasels out.
The weakling is at the front.
The uniform of the day is simply patience.
the highest decoration is the pathos of a star
of hope above the heart.

It is awarded
when nothing happens,
when the drum finale of the artillery falls silent,
when the enemy has become invisible,
when the eternal armament's shadow
darkens the heaven.

It is awarded
for deserting the flag.
For courage in the face of a friend.
For betraying the secrets that shame us.
For the absolute disregard
of any and every order.

## Botschaft

Aus der leichenwarmen Vorhalle des Himmels tritt die
    Sonne.
Es sind dort nicht die Unsterblichen,
sondern die Gerfallenen, vernemehen wir.

Und Glanz kehrt sicht nicht an Verwesung. Unsere
    Gottheit,
die Geschichte, hat uns ein Grab bestellt,
aus dem es keine Auferstehung gibt.

## Message

Out steps the sun,
out of the corpse-warmed entrance hall to the sky.
What we perceive there is not the immortals,
but the fallen.

And what does brilliance care for decay? History is
our God and has ordered us a grave
from which there is no resurrection.

## Die gestundete Zeit

Es kommen härtere Tage.
Die auf Widerruf gestundete Zeit
wird sichtbar am Horizont.
Bald mußt du den Schuh schnüren
und die Hunde zurückjagen in die Marschhöfe.
Denn die Eingeweide der Fische
sind kalt geworden im Wind.
Ärmlich brennt das Licht der Lupinen.
Dein Blick spurt im Nebel:
die auf Widerruf gestundete Zeit
wird sichtbar am Horizont.

Drüben versinkt dir die Geliebte im Sand,
er steigt um ihr wehendes Haar,
er fällt ihr ins Wort,
er befiehlt ihr zu schweigen,
er findet sie sterblich
und willig dem Abschied
nach jeder Umarmung.

Sieh dich nicht um.
Schnür deinen Schuh.
Jag die Hunde zurück.
Wirf die Fische ins Meer.
Lösch die Lupinen!

Es kommen härtere Tage.

## Borrowed Time

Harder days are coming.
That borrowed time
will be due on the horizon.
Soon you must tie your boots
and herd the dogs back to the marshlands,
to the farms. For the fish guts
have grown cold in the wind.
The lupin-lights burn only dimly.
Your eyes track through fog: you see
how borrowed time
will be due on the horizon.

Over there your own beloved sinks into the sand.
It's rising to her windblown hair.
It cuts short her speech.
It orders her to be silent.
It finds out that she is only mortal
and ready and willing to leave
after every embrace.

Don't look round.
Lace your boots.
Drive the dogs back.
Throw the fish into the sea.
Extinguish the lupins!

Harder days are coming.

## Dunkles zu sagen

Wie Orpheus spiel ich
auf den Saiten des Lebens den Tod
und in die Schönheit der Erde
und deiner Augen, die den Himmel verwalten,
weiß ich nur Dunkles zu sagen.

Vergiß nicht, daß auch du, plötzlich,
an jenem Morgen, als dein Lager
noch naß war von Tau und die Nelke
an deinem Herzen schlief,
den dunklen Fluß sahst,
der an dir vorbeizog.

Die Saite des Schweigens
gespannt auf die Welle von Blut,
griff ich dein tönendes Herz.
Verwandelt ward deine Locke
ins Schattenhaar der Nacht,
der Finsternis schwarze Flocken
beschneiten dein Antlitz.

Und ich gehör dir nicht zu.
Beide klagen wir nun.

Aber wie Orpheus weiß ich
auf der Seite des Todes das Leben
und mir blaut
dein für immer geschlossenes Aug.

## To Speak of Dark Things

I am like Orpheus: I play
death on the strings of life,
and to the loveliness of this earth
and to your eyes, which rule the heavens,
I can only speak of dark things.

Don't forget how, all of a sudden,
on that morning when your camp
was still wet with dew, and a carnation
lay asleep on your heart, you also
witnessed the dark river
swiftly rushing past you.

The string of silence
strained on the blood-tide,
I seized your beating heart.
Your curls were transformed
into nighttime's shadowy hair,
your features snowed in
by black flakes of darkness.

And I do not belong to you.
Now both of us lament.

But I am like Orpheus and I know
life on the strings of death
and the becoming-blue
of your eye, forever closed.

## Herbstmanöver

Ich sage nicht: das war gestern. Mit wertlosem
Sommergeld in den Taschen liegen wir wieder
auf der Spreu des Hohns, im Herbstmanöver der Zeit.
Und der Fluchtweg nach Süden kommt uns nicht,
wie den Vögeln, zustatten. Vorüber, am Abend,
ziehen Fischkutter und Gondeln, und manchmal
trifft mich ein Splitter traumsatten Marmors,
wo ich verwundbar bin, durch Schönheit, im Aug.

In den Zeitungen lese ich viel von der Kälte
und ihren Folgen, von Törichten und Toten,
von Vertriebenen, Mördern und Myriaden
von Eisschollen, aber wenig, was mir behagt.
Warum auch? Vor dem Bettler, der mittags kommt,
schlag ich die Tür zu, denn es ist Frieden
und man kann sich den Anblick ersparen, aber nicht
im Regen das freudlose Sterben der Blätter.

Laßt uns eine Reise tun! Laßt uns unter Zypressen
oder auch unter Palmen in den Orangenhainen
zu verbilligten Preisen Sonnenuntergänge sehen,
die nicht ihresgleichen haben! Laßt uns die
unbeantworteten Briefe an das Gestern vergessen!
Die Zeit tut Wunder. Kommt sie uns aber unrecht,
mit dem Pochen der Schuld: wir sind nicht zu Hause.
Im Keller des Herzens, schlaflos, find ich mich wieder
auf der Spreu des Hohns, im Herbstmanöver der Zeit.

## Autumn Maneuver

It's not as if I say—*that was then*. Worthless summer cash
fills our pockets. We lie down again
on the chaff of scorn, in the Autumn maneuver of time.
It's no help to us—that escape to the south
the birds do so easily. In the evening
fishing trawlers, gondolas go past and by-and-by
a sliver of dream-rich marble pierces me
where I am vulnerable, through beauty, in the eye.

I read much in the papers about the cold
and all its consequence. About fools and the dead.
About exiles. Murderers. A myriad
of ice floes. But there is very little that consoles.
Why should it be otherwise? When the beggar comes at
     noon
I slam the door in his face: this is the time of peace
and you can spare yourself that unpleasant sight
but not the joyless dying of the leaves in the rain.

Let's go on a trip! Under the cypress trees
or under the palms or orange groves
let's sit and watch the sunsets—
cut-price and incomparable! And let's forget
the unanswered letters to yesterday.
Time works wonders. But if it calls at the wrong moment,
and with a guilty knock, we're not at home.
Sleepless, in the cellar of the heart, I find myself again
on the chaff of scorn, in the Autumn maneuver of time.

## Abschied von England

Ich habe deinen Boden kaum betreten,
schweigsames Land, kaum einen Stein berührt,
ich war von deinem Himmel so hoch gehoben,
so in Wolken, Dunst und in noch Ferneres gestellt,
daß ich dich schon verließ,
als ich vor Anker ging.

Du hast meine Augen geschlossen
mit Meerhauch und Eichenblatt,
von meinen Tränen begossen,
hieltst du die Gräser satt;
aus meinen Träumen gelöst,
wagten sich Sonnen heran,
doch alles war wieder fort,
wenn dein Tag begann.
Alles blieb ungesagt.

Durch die Straßen flatterten die großen grauen Vögel
und wiesen mich aus.
War ich je hier?

Ich wollte nicht gesehen werden.

Meine Augen sind offen.
Meerhauch und Eichenblatt?
Unter den Schlangen des Meers
seh ich, an deiner Statt,
das Land meiner Seele erliegen.

Ich habe seinen Boden nie betreten.

## Departure from England

Silent land—
I have hardly stepped on your soil.
I have hardly troubled a stone of it.
I was raised so high by your skies and so held
inside your clouds, your hazy mists, your further distances
that I had already left you
before I dropped anchor.

You have shut my eyes
with your sea breezes, your oak leaf.
You let the grasses feed
on the tears I wept.
Released from my dreams, suns
dared to make their way across country.
But everything disappeared
as soon as your day started.
And everything stayed unsaid.

Huge gray birds fluttered down the streets.
They wanted to drive me out.
But was I ever here?

I didn't want to be seen.

My eyes are wide open.
Sea breezes? Oak leaf?
Under the sinuous waves
instead of you I see
the country of my soul give up the ghost.

I have never stepped on its soil.

## Früher Mittag

Still grünt die Linde im eröffneten Sommer,
weit aus den Städten gerückt, flirrt
der mattglänzende Tagmond. Schon ist Mittag,
schon regt sich im Brunnen der Strahl,
schon hebt sich unter den Scherben
des Märchenvogels geschundener Flügel,
und die vom Steinwurf entstellte Hand
sinkt uns erwachende Korn.

Wo Deutschlands Himmel die Erde schwärzt,
sucht sein enthaupteter Engel ein Grab für den Haß
und reicht dir die Schüssel des Herzens.

Eine Handvoll Schmerz verliert sich über den Hügel.

Sieben Jahre später
fällt es dir wieder ein,
am Brunnen vor dem Tore,
blick nicht zu tief hinein,
die Augen gehen dir über.

Siben Jahre später,
in einem Totenhaus,
trinken die Henker von gestern
den goldenen Becher aus.
Die Augen täten dir sinken.

Schon ist Mittag in der Asche
krümmt sich das Eisen, auf den Dorn
ist die Fahne gehißt, und auf den Felsen

## Early Noon

Silently the linden grows green as summer gets near.
The dull gleam of the daylight moon
flickers faraway from cities.
                      Already it's noon.
Already sunlight plays in the fountain.
Already beneath the debris
is lifted the legendary bird's broken wing.
The hand that's in a rictus from throwing stones
sinks into the waking corn.

Where Germany's sky blackens the earth
its beheaded angel
is trying to find a grave for hatred
and offers you
the bowl of the heart.

A handful of pain disappears over the hill.

Seven years on
it all comes back to you
at the fountain in front of the gateway.
Don't look too closely inside:
your eyes fill up with tears.

Seven years on
inside a morgue
the golden cup is drained
by the hangmen of yesterday:
Your eyes look down in shame.

uralten Traums bleibt fortan
der Adler geschmiedet.

Nur die Hoffnung kauert erblindet im Licht.

Lös ihr die Fessel, führ sie
die Halde herab, leg ihr
die Hand auf das Aug, daß sie
kein Schatten versengt!

Wo Deutschlands Erde den Himmel schwärzt,
sucht die Wolke nach Worten und füllt den Krater mit
      Schweigen,
eh sie der Sommer im schütteren Regen vernimmt.

Das Unsägliche geht, leise gesagt, übers Land:
schon ist Mittag.

Already it's noon and in the ashes
iron bends, the flag is run up
on the thorn, and onto the rockface
of an age-old dream the eagle from now on
is welded forever.

Only hope cowers. Is blinded in the light.

Undo its fetters, lead it
down the mountain, put your hand
over its eyes so that
it's not singed by the shadows!

Where Germany's earth blackens the sky
a cloud tries to find words and fills the crater with
            silence
before the summer can realize its lack of rain.

The unspeakable passes, in an undertone, over the land:
already it's noon.

## Exil

Ein Toter bin ich der wandelt
gemeldet nirgends mehr
unbekannt im Reich des Präfekten
überzählig in den goldenen Städten
und im grünenden Land

abgetan lange schon
und mit nichts bedacht

Nur mit Wind mit Zeit und mit Klang
der ich unter Menschen nicht leben kann

Ich mit der deutschen Sprache
dieser Wolke um mich
die ich halte als Haus
treibe durch alle Sprachen

O wie sie sich verfinstert
die dunklen die Regentöne
nur die wenigen fallen

In hellere Zonen trägt dann sie den Toten hinauf

## Exile

I am a dead man.
A wandering man.
Unregistered anywhere.
Unseen on the bureaucrat's radar.
Unknown in the cities of gold
or the greening countryside.

They washed their hands of me
a long time ago.
I was provided with nothing—

only with wind only with time only with sound

I am one who cannot live among my own kind

Now with the German language —
my cloud cover
which I keep as a roof over my head—
I drift through all languages.

Oh, how it darkens!
Those muted tones, those rainy ones!
only a few fall—

It will carry up the dead to a world of light.

## Ihr Worte

*(Für Nelly Sachs, die Freundin, die Dichterin, in Verehrung)*

Ihr Worte, auf, mir nach!,
und sind wir auch schon weiter,
zu weit gegangen, geht's noch einmal
weiter, zu keinem Ende geht's.

Es hellt nicht auf.

Das Wort
wird doch nur
andre Worte nach sich ziehn,
Satz den Satz.
So möchte Welt,
endgültig,
sich aufdrängen,
schon gesagt sein.
Sagt sie nicht.

Worte, mir nach,
daß nicht endgültig wird
—nicht diese Wortbegier
und Spruch auf Widerspruch!

Laßt eine Weile jetzt
keins der Gefühle sprechen,
den Muskel Herz
sich anders üben.

Laßt, sag ich, laßt.

# You Words

(For Nelly Sachs, friend and poet, with reverence)

Get up words! Get up and follow me —
and although we've already gone too far,
and gone farther, once more it goes
farther and goes forever.

It does not become clearer.

The word
will only drag
other words behind it,
the sentence a sentence.
This is the way
the world wishes
to plead its own cause —
to be said, to be spoken:
Do not speak.

Words
come and follow me
so that nothing will be finalized —
neither the passion for a word,
nor a saying, nor a counter-saying.

And just for now
let no feeling speak about itself.
Let the heart's muscle
exercise in some other way.

Let it be, I say. Let it rest.

Ins höchste Ohr nicht,
nichts, sag ich, geflüstert,
zum Tod fall dir nichts ein,
laß, und mir nach, nicht mild
noch bitterlich,
nicht trostreich,
ohne Trost
bezeichnend nicht,
so auch nicht zeichenlos—

Und nur nicht dies: das Bild
im Staubgespinst, leeres Geroll
von Silben, Sterbenswörter.

Kein Sterbenswort,
Ihr Worte!

And so I say: whisper,
nothing
into the highest ear.
Don't brood about death.
Let it be. And follow me. And be
neither mild mannered
nor bitter
nor comforting—
without consolation,
without import,
and therefore not without symbolism—

Above all, not this: the image
dusted with cobwebs, the vacant rumbling—
syllables, dying words.

Not a dying word—
you words!

# Marie Luise Kaschnitz

1901–1974

# A BIOGRAPHICAL NOTE

*Marie Luise Kaschnitz* was born in January 1901 as Marie Luise Freiin von Holzing-Berstett in southwest Germany at the northern edge of the Black Forest. Her first home was on the estate of her aristocratic family in Karlsruhe. Her father was an officer in the Imperial army. Shortly after her birth, they moved to Potsdam.

Just a year before World War I the family moved again to Berlin, where she went to school. Following the separation of her parents after the war—and seeking independence from her family—she became a bookseller in Weimar in 1917.

In 1924 she worked as a secretary in the Archaeological Institute in Rome. Here she met her future husband the Austrian archaeologist Guido Baron von Kaschnitz-Weinberg. They married in 1925. It was a marriage that was exceptionally close, if nomadic, until his death in 1958.

Her only child, Iris Costanza, was born in 1928. From then on, she and her husband traveled extensively. They visted North Africa and southern Europe. They lived in many places, although Frankfurt and Rome constituted their two real homes. From 1926 to 1932 as well as from 1953 to 1956 they lived in Rome; from 1932 to 1937 in Konigsberg. From 1937 to 1941 they were in Marburg. Finally from 1941 to 1953 they were in Frankfurt.

In the 1940s the family was trapped in the firebombings of

Frankfurt. The images and impressions from those years of war became a strong presence in Kaschnitz's work. One of her darkest poems, "Hiroshima," which is included here, is an exploration of the brutality and anonymity of bombing.

Her first book, a novel, *Liebe beginnt*, was published in 1933. In 1947, just after the war, she published *Totentanz und Gedichte zur Zeit. Neue Gedichte* was published in 1957. *Dein Schweigen, meine Stimme* (Your Silence, My Voice) was published in 1962 after the death of her husband (an event which devastated her and for a while caused her seclusion even from writing). *Ein Wort Weiter* (One Word Further) was published in 1965 and *Kein Zauberspruch* (No Magic Formula) her last book, was published postuhumously in 1974.

In 1955 she received the Georg-Buchner-Preis. She died in Rome in 1974 and is buried at her family's estate in Germany.

## Hiroshima

Der den Tod auf Hiroshima warf
Ging ins Kloster, läutet dort die Glocken.
Der den Tod auf Hiroshima warf
Sprang vom Stuhl in die Schlinge, erwürgte sich.
Der den Tod auf Hiroshima warf
Fiel in Wahnsinn, wehrt Gespenster ab
Hunderttausend, die ihn angehen nächtlich
Auferstandene aus Staub für ihn.

Nichts von alledem ist wahr.
Erst vor kurzem sah ich ihn
Im Garten seines Hauses vor der Stadt.
Die Hecken waren noch jung und die Rosenbüsche
	zierlich.
Das wächst nicht so schnell, daß sich einer verbergen
	könnte
Im Wald des Vergessens. Gut zu sehen war
Das nackte Vorstadthaus, die junge Frau
Die neben ihm stand im Blumenkleid
Das kleine Mädchen an ihrer Hand
Der Knabe der auf seinem Rücken saß
Und über seinem Kopf die Peitsche schwang.
Sehr gut erkennbar war er selbst
Vierbeinig auf dem Grasplatz, das Gesicht
Verzerrt von Lachen, weil der Photograph
Hinter der Hecke stand, das Auge der Welt.

## Hiroshima

The man who dropped death on Hiroshima
Rings bells in the cloister, has taken vows.
The man who dropped death on Hiroshima
Put his head in a noose and hanged himself.
The man who dropped death on Hiroshima
Is out of his mind, is battling with risen souls
Made of atomic dust who are out to attack him.
Every night. Hundreds and thousands of them.

None of it's true.
In fact, I saw him the other day
In his front garden, there in the suburb—
With immature hedges and dainty roses.
You need time to make a Forest of Forgetting
Where someone can hide. Plainly on view
Was the naked, suburban house and the young wife
Standing beside him in her floral dress
And the little girl attached to her hand
And the boy hoisted up on his back
And cracking a whip over his head.
And he was easy to pick out
On all fours there on the lawn, his face
Contorted with laughter, because the photographer
        stood
Behind the hedge, the seeing eye of the world.

## Selinunte

Was sie vom Krieg erzählen, von den Tausend
Zerstörten Städten, überrascht mich nicht.
Gott hat die sechzig Säulen des Tempels C
Auf einmal umgeworfen. Er hat dazu
Keine Bomben und keine schweren Geschütze
       gebraucht
Nur einen einzigen tieferen Atemzug.

Fremde kommen, wenn die Mandelwälder
Blühen, viele über den Hügel.
Die Sonne blitzt in ihren Windschutzscheiben.
Nicht nach Schafwolle riechen sie, nicht nach Erde
Ihre Kleider fühlen sich an wie gesponnenes Glas.
Keiner weiß, wie das ist, wenn der Abend kommt
Wenn die letzten Scheinwerfer hinter den Bergen
       verschwinden
Wie dann die einsamen Hunde bellen landüber
Wie unter den Sternen die Grillen schreien.

Mein kleiner Bruder hüpft im hölzernen Ställchen.
Die roten Lilien auf der Wachstuchdecke
Tanzen im Schimmer der Petroleumlampe.
Mein Vater sucht den schwangeren Schoß
Meiner gelben, verwelkten Mutter
An die verbrannte Kuste schhägt das Meer.

Wenn mein Bräutigam ruft, der Lammträger, zittere ich.
Wasser gehen wir holen vom Brunnen der Totengöttin
Er preßt seinen Mund auf meinen Mund.
Niemals werd ich die gläsernen Nachtstädte sehen
Sagt die Tochter des Wächters von Selinunt.

## Selinunte

I'm not surprised at what they tell
when they tell of the war:
To hear about thousands of cities destroyed.
God blew down the sixty pillars
Of Temple C just like that.
No need for bombs. No need for artillery.
Just one deep breath.

Strangers come over the hill
When the almond groves come into flower.
The sun gleams in their windscreens.
They don't smell of sheep's wool, nor of dirt.
Their clothes feel like spun glass.
No one knows what it's like when evening comes,
When the last headlights disappear behind mountains.
How the lonely dogs bark far away.
How the crickets shriek under the stars.

My little brother plays in the wooden shed.
Red lilies on the oilcloth
Dance by the light of the oil lamp.
My father seeks out the pregnant shape
Of my yellowish, withered mother.
The ocean batters the burned-out coast.

I shake when my bridegroom, the shepherd, calls.
We go to the well of the goddess of death for water.
He presses his mouth to my mouth.
I will never see the night cities of glass
Says the watchman's daughter of Selinunte.

## Nicht mutig

Die Mutigen wissen
Daß sie nicht auferstehen
Daß kein Fleisch um sie wächst
Am jüngsten Morgen
Daß sie nichts mehr erinnern
Niemandem wiederbegegnen
Daß nichts ihrer wartet
Keine Seligkeit
Keine Folter
Ich
Bin nicht mutig.

## Not Brave

The brave know
They will not rise again
That no flesh will grow around them
On Judgment Morning
That they won't remember anything
That they won't see anyone ever again
That nothing of theirs is waiting
No salvation
No torture
I
Am not brave.

# Hilde Domin

1909–

# A BIOGRAPHICAL NOTE

*Hilde Domin* was born as Hildegard Löwenstein, daughter of a Jewish lawyer, in Cologne in 1909. Her home was not Orthodox and she herself has stated that she considered herself, at least to begin with, as an assimilated German Jew. She began her studies in Cologne, then moved on to the Universities of Heidelberg and Berlin where she studied philosophy and political science. She worked on her dissertation with Karl Mannheim and Karl Jaspers.

In 1932, as anti-Semitism was becoming institutionalized in Germany, she decided to leave her own country and seek shelter in Italy. Initially, she went to Florence. Her parents remained in Cologne for another year. In 1933 they followed their daughter into flight from the Nazi regime; in their case they selected England as a sanctuary.

She finished her dissertation on a precursor of Machiavelli at the University of Florence, earning a Dott. Scienze Politiche. She married Erwin Walter Palm in Italy in 1936 and lived with him in Rome, teaching languages there, until 1939. At one point they barely escaped capture in a Fascist roundup of Jews in Rome.

They left for England in 1939 to join her parents. She taught there for a year but could not settle. Despite the fact that she had not been a direct victim of the Nazis, Hilde Domin's fear that Hitler would conquer all of Europe was acute. She left England with her husband in 1940 and settled in Santo Domingo in the Dominican Republic for more than a decade, where both she and her husband were teachers.

In 1950 and 1951 both her parents died. Hilde Domin has spoken of the death of her mother as a defining event: "it is a fact that 'my second life,' the life of the poet Domin, started after her death" and this "was one of the events which shook my life at the time." Three years later she returned to Heidelberg with Erwin Palm. From then on, with the exception of a year in Spain, she made her life in Heidelberg, Germany. In 1959 she published her first volume of poetry *Nur eine Rose als Stütze* (Only One Rose As Support). In 1964 she published an acclaimed volume of poetry *Hier* (Here). She published *Aber die Hoffnung: Autobiographisches aus und über Deutschland* (Yet Hope: Autobiographies of and from Germany) in 1982. Also *Ich will dich* (I Want You) in 1970.

She has received many honors. In 1983 she received the Nelly-Sachs-Preis der Stadt Dortmund. Today she lives in Heidelberg.

*Köln*

Die versunkene Stadt
für mich
allein
versunken.

Ich schwimme
in diesen Straßen.
Andere gehn.

Die alten Häuser
haben neue große Türen
aus Glas.

Die Toten und ich
wir schwimmen
durch die neuen Türen
unserer alten Häuser.

## Cologne

The sunken city,
sunken
for me
alone.

I swim
in these streets.
Others walk.

The old houses
have grand, new doors,
all of glass.

We swim,
the dead and I,
through the new doors
of our old houses.

## Geburtstage

### 1
Sie ist tot

heute ist ihr Geburtstag
das ist der Tag
an dem sie
in diesem Dreieck
zwischen den Beinen ihrer Mutter
herausgewürgt wurde
sie
die mich herausgewürgt hat
zwischen ihren Beinen
sie ist Asche

\*

Immer denke ich
an die Geburt eines Rehs
wie es die Beine auf den Boden setzte

\*

Ich habe niemand ins Licht gezwängt
nur Worte
Worte drehen nicht den Kopf
sie stehen auf
sofort
und gehn

## Birthdays

1
She is dead

today is her birthday
this is the day
on which
in this triangle
she was pushed out
between the legs of her mother
she
who pushed me out
between her legs

she is ash

*

I always think
of the birth of a deer
how it puts its legs to the ground.

*

I have pushed no one into the light
only words
Words do not turn their head
they stand up
at once
and walk away

## Exil

Der sterbende Mund
müht sich
um das richtig gesprochene
Wort
einer fremden
Sprache.

## Exile

The mouth dying
The mouth twisted
The mouth trying
to say the word right
in a strange language.

# Dagmar Nick

1926–

# A BIOGRAPHICAL NOTE

*Dagmar Nick* was born in 1926 in Breslau, in East Germany, a city on the River Oder, which is now Wrocław in Poland. Her household was artistic and musical. Her father Edmund Nick was a composer and her mother Kaete Nick-Jaenicke was both an actress and a singer.

In 1933 she moved to Berlin. She studied Psychology and Graphology at Munich University. Her first poems were published in Erich Kästner's postwar journal *Neuen Zeitung* in 1945.

Her first book *Märtyrer* (Martyr) was published in 1947. In 1955 she published *Das Buch Holofernes* (The Book of Holfernes). This was followed in 1959 by *In den Ellipsen des Mondes* (In the Eclipse of the Moon). *Zeugnis und Zeichen* (Summons and Sign) was published in 1969 and has been translated in its entirety by the American poet, Jim Barnes, as has *Gezählte Tage* (Numbered Days), published in 1986.

Among her prizes are the Liliencron-Preis der Stadt Hamburg (1948), the Eichendorff-Preis (1966), the Ehrengabe zum Andreas-Gryphius-Preis (1970), Roswitha-von-Gandersheim-Medaille (1977), the Kulturpreis Schlesien des Landes Niedersachsen (1986), and the Jakob-Wassermann-Literaturpreis (2002). Her most recent books are a selected poems: *Wegmarken: Ausgewählte Gedichte* and *Liebesgedichte* (Love Poems) (2001).

She has been described as being, with Ingeborg Bachmann, Rose Ausländer, and Hilde Domin, among the most important German-speaking poets since 1945.

## Flugwetter

Die Himmel dröhnen
Vergeltung.
Bin Scwalbenwirbel
im Sog der Gefahr
ruft das Chaos aus.

Wir üben das Sterben ein
mit dem Schleudersitz
täglich und täglich.

Zweihundert Meter und
ein Grab tiefer:
wie tröstlich
das rote Kreuz auf dem Dach.

Wir kennen die keimfreien
Messer, den neuen OP
und die Riten
der letzen Ölung.
Manchmal erkennen wir beides
zu spät.

## Flying Weather

The heavens drone
their revenge.
Swallows eddying
in the wake of danger
cry out Chaos.

Day after day,
we rehearse our deaths
in the ejection seat.

Two hundred meters
and one grave deeper:
How comforting it is,
the red cross on the roof.

We know the sterile
scalpels, the new OR.
We know the rites
of Extreme Unction.
Sometimes we recognize both
too late.

## Aufruf

Die Feldzeichen stehen auf Mord.
In den letzten Waldreservaten
patrouillieren Rudel von Wölfen.
Schlagt eine Schneise!
Laßt sie herein!
Laßt die Wölfe ins Blut!

## Summons

The banners are signaling murder.
In the last preserved forests
the wolf packs are out on patrol.
Clear a space for them!
Let them come in!
Let the wolves at the blood!

## Den Generälen ins Soldbuch

Ordnet die Himmel neu,
ihr Herrscher der Heerscharen,
setzt den Monden,
die ihr mit euren Sonden beleidigt,
neue Gezeiten,
teilt die Sonnensysteme
unter euch auf,
ihr braucht Raum für die Toten,
fügt ins Sternbild der Zwietracht
den Kainsstern, das Brudermal,
Grabmal für einen und tausend Gemordete,
der Messias wird euch nicht hindern,
künftige Stahlsärge
in den Staub der Planeten zu senken
im Namen der Väter und der Söhne
und der geheiligten Hybris,
ordnet die Himmel neu,
die uns verheißen sind,
aber vergeßt nicht die Hölle,
ihr Herrscher der Heerscharen,
eine neue Hölle für uns,
die wir zu überleben hofften
am Rande des Chaos.

## In the Book of the Generals

Make a new order in the Heavens,
you lords of the legions.
And that moon
you affront with your soundings,
set new tides for it.
Divide the solar systems
up among you:
you need that space for the dead.
Take the star of Cain, mark of the brother,
and fit it into the constellation Discord—
a monument to the one and thousand slaughtered.
The Messiah will not hinder you
from lowering future coffins of steel
into planetary dust
in the name of the Fathers and the Sons
and the holy Hybris.
Make a new order in the Heavens
that are promised to us.
But, you lords of the legions,
don't forget hell—
our new hell
which we had hoped to survive
on the edge of Chaos.

## Niemandsland

Wo die Landschaft nicht aufhört
Himmel zu sein,
wo unsere Schatten sich
anrühren
Nacht für Nacht
mit gefesselten Flügeln
auf dem schmalen Grat
zwischen Drüben und Hier,
wo wir sind
und nicht sind,
traumlos und ohne Gewähr
im Bannkreis des Blutes—
liegen wir
an den pulsenden Ufern,
geschlagen und unter
gefällten Standarten—
Ohnmacht und Schuld.

## No-Man's-Land

Where the landscape dissolves
into sky,
where night after night
our shadows
touch each other
with fettered wings
on the narrow ridge
between here and there,
between where we are
and where we are not—
in a cursed circle of blood,
our dreams gone and no guarantees—
we lie on the pulsing shore
battered and beneath
our fallen banners—
Powerlessness. Guilt.

## An Abel

Mein toter Rivale Abel,
wohlgefällig im Dunst
deiner Widderkadaver,
du Erstgeburtenverschleuderer,
hast du Rachegelüste
und schließt em Komplott
mit dem rauchfahnenflüchtigen Gott
ohne Namen?

Was soll diese Gnade,
mich an deiner Statt
Geschlechter zeugen zu lassen,
Mörder um Mörder,
die das Blutopfer lieben
wie du?
Was soll diese Gnade?

## To Abel

Abel, my dead rival,
you firstborn, good-for-nothing,
how well you please with the smoke rising
from your Aries-like cadaver.
Have you lusted for revenge,
have you entered into a plot
with a God as fleeting as smoke—
trails, a God without a name?

What is the meaning of this mercy?
To leave me here in your stead
to beget the race—
murderer upon murderer—
who love the blood sacrifice
just as much as you?
What can this mercy mean?

## Emigration

Altes Europa,
Totenland, das uns zum Sterben aufnimmt
an jedem Abend;
im Schiaf der Verbannten
ist noch dein Aschenflügel zu spüren,
nachtatmende Trauer um
Fortgegebenes
und die Brandspur unter der Haut,
mit der wir dahinzogen,
altes Europa, Wunschland,
das uns entwurzelte
und dem wir doch niemals entgehen,
eingeboren in dein Gesicht,
deine Herbste und Dämmerungen,
gesiegelt von deiner Vergangenheit,
die uns verfolgt bis in die Morgenstunde,
wenn wir erwachen, traumoffen,
gebrochenen Mutes,
die Hoffnung auf Halbmast.

# Emigration

Old Europe,
land of the dead, which every evening
gathers us in to die —
still your wings of ash leave their tracks
in the exile's sleep.
A dark breath of lament
for what we lost, and
a brand of fire under our skin,
has been with us as we wandered.
Old Europe,
land of our desire,
you have dragged us up by our roots,
yet we can never escape you —
born as we are to countenance
your autumns and your half-lights,
sealed in as we are by your past:
it hunts us down into the first hours of the morning,
as we awake, open to our dreams,
our spirits crushed,
our hopes fluttering at half mast.

# NOTES

ROSE AUSLÄNDER: "BIOGRAPHICAL NOTE"
*extinguished by / the Pruth.*
The Pruth is a tributary of the Danube River, and the boundary of Romania with Moldova. It rises on the northeastern slopes of the Eastern Carpathians in southwestern Ukraine and flows 530 miles (850 km) north, then east. It flows past Rose Ausländer's native city of Czernowitz on its way south-southeast. It empties into the Danube east of Galați, Romania.

ELISABETH LANGGÄSSER: "SPRING 1946"
Elisabeth Langgasser's daughter, whose return is celebrated in *Frühling 1946*, was Cordelia Heller, later Cordelia Edvardson. In her memoir *Burned Child Seeks the Fire* she complicates and harrows the poem with an account of her mother and herself, in Gestapo headquarters, confronting the inevitability of the daughter's deportation to Auschwitz.

> Uncertainly, the daughter looked at the mother, and her gaze met with a white mask in which the overly red mouth burned like a wound. No support could be expected from the mother at this moment, the girl immediately realized that. A great fear befell her, but as always, defiance came to her aid. Oh no, not so fast, and not the *Judenstern* again. Removal to the East didn't sound so good either, but she had had her experiences with the *Judenstern*. The girl decided to play the cheeky Berlin girl, a part she had created on past occasions with considerable

151

success. May I please call my embassy: she said to the official, and found the sound of that quite grown-up and impressive. After all, he had addressed her with *Sie*. There was a flash in the eyes behind the spectacles, and the moustache twitched with suppressed laughter: Why, certainly, Miss, here is the telephone! Obligingly he picked up the telephone and put it in front of her, and her hand was already on the receiver when he continued, and now the dragon spit fire: *But*, and the word sounded like the crack of a whip, but if you do not sign on the spot, we will have to prosecute your mother! He told the girl that the mother had arranged the daughter's Spanish adoption in order to circumvent German laws, which could be regarded as a serious offense, as treason, high treason, and some third category which the girl was later unable to remember. However, if the girl signed now, no harm would be done, and the mother's lapse could be excused. And he added, just to be sure: You are no doubt aware of the fact that your mother is a half-Jew. Again the daughter looked at the mother and met with the gaze of her beautiful brown eyes, eyes that shone with intensity, that knew how to cast a spell on the girl, but which now were full to the brim with wordless, helpless pain. No one said anything, nothing needed to be said, there was no choice, there never had been, she was Cordelia, who kept her vow of fidelity, she was also Proserpine, she was the chosen one, and never had she felt closer to her mother's heart. Her voice was choked, but finally she got the words out: Yes, I'll sign?

> *(From* Burned Child Seeks the Fire *by Cordelia Edvardson, trans. Joel Agee [Beacon Press, 1998])*


MARIE LUISE KASCHNITZ: "SELINUNTE"

Selinunte is a modern Greek town on the southern coast of Italy. Nearby are the ruins of Selinus, an ancient Greek city It was founded by colonists from Megara in the fifth century B.C. Its Doric temples—the largest, Temple G, was the fourth largest Greek temple ever built—were destroyed in 409 B.C. in a siege by the Carthaginians.

# CHECKLISTS

ROSE AUSLÄNDER
*Originating Volumes*
*Blinder Sommer. Gedichte.* Vienna: Bergland Verlag, 1965.
Am Ende der Zeit
Meine Nachtigall
Im Chagall-Dorf
Mein Schlüssel
*36 Gerechte.* Hamburg: Hoffman und Campe Verlag, 1967.
Verwundert
*Mutterland: Gedichte.* Cologne: Braun, 1978.
Mutterland
*Noch ist Raum: Gedichte.* Duisburg: Gilles & Francke Verlag, 1976.
Damit kein Licht uns liebe
Biographische Notiz
*Books by Rose Ausländer in German*
*Der Regenbogen.* Poems. Czernowitz: Verlag Literaria, 1939.
*Blinder Sommer.* Poems. Vienna: Bergland-Verlag, 1965.
*36 Gerechte:* Gedichte. Hamburg: Hoffman & Campe, 1967.
*Ohne Visum.* Poems and short prose. Düsseldorf: Sassfras
    Verlag, 1974.
*Andere Zeichen.* Poems. Concept-Verlag, Düsseldorf: 1975.
*Gesammelte Gedichte.* Hugo Käufer and Berndt Mosblech,
    eds., Braun, Cologne: 1978.

153

*Gesammelte Werke in acht Bänden.* Helmut Braun, ed.
Fischer, Frankfurt: 1984–1990.
*The Forbidden Tree: Englische Gedichte.* Helmut Braun, ed.
Fischer, 1995.
*Rose Ausländer: Materialien zu Leben und Werk.* Frankfurt:
Fischer (Tb.), 1992.
*Wir wohnen in Babylon: Gedichte.* Fischer, 1992.
Sources in English
Ausländer, Rose. *Selected Poems: Rose Ausländer:* Ewald Osers
trans. London: Magazine Editions, 1977.
——. *An Ark of Stars: Poems by Rose Ausländer* Fischer
Taschenbuch Verlag, 1990.
——. *Mother Tongue: Selected Poems. Rose Ausländer:* Jean
Boase-Beier and Anthony Vivis trans., London: Arc Books,
1995.
Bower, Kathrin M. *Ethics and Remembrance in the Poetry of
Nelly Sachs and Rose Ausländer:* Rochester: Camden
House, 2000.

ELISABETH LANGGÄSSER
*Originating Volumes*
*Mithras Lyrik und Prosa.* Fischer: Frankfurt am Main 1959.
Frühling 1946
*Books by Elisabeth Langgässer in German*
*Der Wendekreis des Lammes.* Gedichte Veröffentlichungen
Auswahl, 1924).
*Die Tierkreisgedichte.* 1935.
*Das unauslöschliche Siegel.* Hamburg: Claassen & Goverts,
1946.
*Der Torso.* Hamburg: Claassen & Goverts, 1947.
*Das Labyrinth: fünf Erzählungen.* Hamburg: Claassen &
Goverts, 1949.
*Proserpina: eine Kindheitsmythe.* 1933; reprint, Hamburg:
Claassen & Goverts, 1933.
*Der Laubmann und die Rose.* Hamburg: Claassen & Goverts,
1947.

*Märkische Argonautenfahrt.* Hamburg: Claassen & Goverts, 1950.

*Sources in English*
Ausländer, Rose. *The Quest.* Jane Bannard Greene, trans. New York: Knopf, 1953.
Edvardson, Cordelia. *Burned Child Seeks the Fire* Joel Agee, trans.: Boston: Beacon Press, 1998.

## NELLY SACHS

*Originating Volumes*
*In den Wohnungen des Todes.* Berlin: Aufbau-Verlag, 1947.
Wenn ich nur wüsste
*Und niemand weiss weiter.* Hamburg: Ellermann, 1957.
Kommt einer von ferne
Bereit sind alle Länder
In der blauen ferne
*Flucht und Verwandlung: Gedichte.* Stuttgart: Deutsche Verlags-Anstalt, 1959.
In der Flucht
*Fahrt ins Staublose. die Gedichte der Nelly Sachs.* Frankfurt am Main: Suhrkamp Verlag, 1961.
In diesem Amethyst

*Books by Nelly Sachs in German*
*Legenden und Erzählungen.* Berlin: F.W. Mayer, 1921.
*In den Wohnungen des Todes.* Berlin: Aufbau-Verlag, 1947.
*Sternverdunkelung,* 1947.
*Und niemand weiss weiter.* Hamburg: Ellermann, 1957.
*Flucht und Verwandlung: Gedichte.* Berlin: Deutsche Verlags-Anstalt, 1959.
*Späte Gedichte.* Frankfurt am Main: Suhrkamp, 1965.
*Gedichte.* Frankfurt am Main: Surhkamp, 1977.

*Books about Nelly Sachs in German*
Dinesen, Ruth. *Nelly Sachs. Eine Biographie.* (Aus dem Dänischen von Gabriele Gerecke) Frankfurt: Suhrkamp, 1994.

Falkenstein, Henning. *Nelly Sachs*. Berlin: Collquium Verlag, 1984.

*Sources in English*

Bower, Kathrin M. *Ethics and Remembrance in the Poetry of Nelly Sachs and Rose Ausländer*. Rochester: Camden House, 2000.

Celan, Paul. *Paul Celan, Nelly Sachs: Correspondence*. Christopher Clark trans. Riverdale-on-Hudson, NY: Sheep Meadow Press, 1995.

Sachs, Nelly. *O the Chimneys: Selected Poems*, including the verse play, Eli. Michael Hamburger, trans. New York: Farrar, Straus and Giroux, 1967.

——. *The Seeker and Other Poems*: Ruth Mead and Matthew Mead, trans. New York: Farrar, Straus and Giroux, 1970.

——. *Selected Poems 1*. Beth Mead and Matthew Mead trans. Los Angeles: Green Integer Books, 2003.


**GERTRUD KOLMAR**

*Originating Volumes*

Gertrud Kolmar: Das Lyrishche Werk. Munich: Kosel Verlag, 1960.

Das Opfer

*Books by and about Gertrud Kolmar in German*

Gedichte. Berlin: Egon Flieschel & Co. 1917.

Die Frau und die Tiere: Gedichte. Berlin: Jüdischer Buchverlag Erwin Löwe, 1938.

Das lyrishche Werk. Munich: Kosel-Verlag, 1960.

Die Kerze von Arras.Gedichte. Berlin: Aufbau Verlag, 1960.

Tag und Tierträume. Munich: Deutsche Taschenbuch Verlag, 1963.

Welten. Frankfurt: Suhrkamp, 1999.

Johanna Woltmann. Gertrud Kolmar, Leben und Werk. Gottingen: Wallstein, 1995.

Johanna Woltmann, ed. *Gertrud Kolmar: Briefe*. Gotttingen: Wallstein, 1997.

*Sources in English*

Frantz, Barbara C. *Gertrud Kolmar's Prose*. New York: Peter Lang Publishing, 1997.

Kolmar, Gertrud. *Dark Soliloquy: The Selected Poems of Gertrud Kolmar*. New York: Seabury, 1975. Henry A. Smith, trans.

——. *A Jewish Mother from Berlin: a Novel; Susanna: a Novella*. Brigitte M. Goldstein, trans. New York: Holmes & Meier Publishers, 1997.

——. *My Gaze Is Turned Inward: Letters 1938–1943*. Northwestern, 2002.

——. *Selected Poems of Gertrud Kolmar:* David Kipp, trans. London: Magpie Press, 1970.


ELSE LASKER-SCHÜLER

*Originating Volumes*

   *Mein blaues Klavier: Neue Gedichte*. Jerusalem· Jerusalem Press, 1943.

      Mein Blaues Klavier

      Ich Weiss

      Herbst

      Abends

      Meine Mutter

      Über glitzerneden Kies

   *Sämlichte Gedichte*. Friedhelm Kemp, ed. Munich: Kösel-Verlag, 1966.

      Ein Einziger Mensch

*Books by Else Lasker-Schüler in German*

   *Styx*. Berlin: Axel Juncker, 1902.

   *Der Siebente Tag*. Berlin: Amelangsche Buchhandlung, 1905.

   *Die Wupper*. Berlin: Oesterheld, 1909.

   *Hebräische Balladen*. Berlin: A. R. Mayer, 1913.

*Der Wunderrabbiner von Barcelona.* Berlin: Paul Cassirer, 1921.
*Konzert.* Berlin: Rowohlt, 1932.
*Das Hebräerland.* Zürich: Oprecht, 1937.
*Mein blaues Klavier: Neue Gedichte.* Jerusalem: Jerusalem
Press Ltd., 1943.
*Sämlichte Gedichte.* Munich: Kösel-Verlag, 1966.
*Briefe von Else Lasker-Schüler.* Munich: Kösel-Verlag, 1969.
*Gesammelte Werke: in acht Bänden.* Munich: Deutsche
Verlags-Anstalt, 1986.
*"Wos sol lich hier."* Exilbriefe an Salman Schocken.
Heidelberg: Verlag Lambert Schneider, 1986.

*Sources in English*

Cohn, Hans W. *Else Lasker-Schüler: The Broken World.*
London: Cambridge University Press, 1974.
Falkenberg, Betty. *Else Lasker-Schüler: A Life.* Jefferson, N.C.:
McFarland & Company, 2003.
Heizer, Donna K. *Jewish-German Identity in the Orientalist
Literature of Else Lasker-Schüler, Friedrich Wolf, and Franz
Werfel.* Columbia, SC: Camden House, 1996.
Jones, Calvin N. *The Literary Reputation of Else Lasker-
Schüler: Criticism 1901–1993.* Columbia, SC: Camden
House, 1994.
Lasker-Schuler, Else. *Concert (Konzert)* (European Women
Writers Ser.) Jean M. Snook, trans. University of Nebraska
Press, 1994.
————. *Hebrew ballads and other poems;* Audri Durchslag and
Jeanette Litman-Demeestère trans., Philadephia: Jewish
Publication Society of America, 1980.
————. *Selected Poems.* Audri Durchslat-Litt and Jeanette
Litman Demeestere trans.: Green Integer Books, 2000.
————. *Star in My Forehead: Selected Poems* Janine Canan,
trans., Duluth, Minn.: Holy Cow Press, 2000.
————. *Your Diamond Dreams Cut Open My Arteries: Poems
by Else Lasker-Schüler* Robert P. Newton, trans. Chapel
Hill: Univ. of North Carolina Press, 1982.

Schwertfeger, Ruth. *Else Lasker-Schüler: Inside This Deathly
Solitude* (Berg Women's Series). New York and Oxford:
Berg, 1991.

Yudkin, Leon I. *Else Lasker-Schüler: A Study in German
Jewish Literature:* Northwood: Science Reviews, 1991.

## INGEBORG BACHMANN

*Originating Volumes*
    *Die gestundete Zeit: Gedichte* 1953; Reprint, Munich: Piper, 1957.
      Alle Tage
      Botschaft
      Die gestundete Zeit
      Dunkles zu sagen
      Herbstmanöver
      Abschied von England
      Früher Mittag
    *Werke 1: Ingeborg Bachmann.* Munich: Piper, 1978.
      Exil
      Ihre Worte

*Books by Ingeborg Bachmann in German*
    *Die kritische Aufnahme der Existenzialphilosophie Martin
    Heideggers* (doctoral dissertation), 1950.

*Ein Geschäft mit Träumen* (radioplay), 1952.

*Anrufung des Großen Bären: Gedichte.* Munich: Piper, 1956.

*Die gestundete Zeit: Gedichte.* 1953. Reprint, Munich: Piper,
1957.

*Das dreißigste Jahr.* Munich: Piper, 1961.

*Der gute Gott von Manhattan: Die Zikaden.* 1958. Munich:
Piper, 1958.

*Jugend in einer Österreichischen Stadt,* 1961.

*Gedichte, Erzählungen Hörspiele, Essays.* Munich: Piper, 1964.

*Malina.* Frankfurt am Main: Suhrkamp, 1971.

*Simultan: neue Erzählungen.* Munich: Piper, 1972.

*Werke 1: Ingeborg Bachmann.* Munich: Piper, 1978.

*Sources in English*

Achberger, Karen R. *Understanding Ingeborg Bachmann.*
Columbia, S.C.: University of South Carolina Press, 1995.

Bachmann, Ingeborg. *In the Storm of Roses: Selected Poems.*
Mark Anderson, trans. and ed. Princeton: Princeton UP, 1986.

———. *Malina.* Philip Boehm, trans. New York: Holmes and
Meier, 1990.

———. *The Thirtieth Year.* Michael Bullock trans. New York:
Holmes and Meier, 1989.

———. *Three Paths to the Lake.* Mary Fran Gilbert. trans.
New York: Holmes and Meier, 1989.

Brokoph-Mauch, Gudrun. *Thunder Rumbling at My Heels:
Tracing Ingeborg Bachmann:* Ariadne Press, 1998.

———. *Songs in Flight: The Collected Poems of Ingeborg
Bachmann,* Peter Filkins, trans. New York: Marsilio Press,
1994.

Ingeborg Bachmann; Christa Wolf Patricia A. Herminghouse,
ed. *Selected Prose and Drama.* New York: Continuum
International Press, 1998.

## MARIE LUISE KASCHNITZ

*Originating Volumes*

*Zukunftsmusik: Gedichte.* Hamburg: Claassen & Goverts, 1950.

Nicht mutig

*Neue Gedichte.* Hamburg: Claassen & Goverts, 1957.

Hiroshima

Selinunte

*Books by and about Marie Luise Kaschnitz in German*

*Liebe Beginnt.* Berlin: Bruno Cassirer, 1933.

*Totentanz und Gedichte zur Zeit:* Hamburg, Claassen &
Goverts, 1947.

*Zukunftsmusik: Gedichte.* Hamburg: Claassen & Goverts,
1950.

*Ewige Stadt: Rom-Gedichte.* Krefeld: Scherpe-Verlag, 1952.

*Neue Gedichte.* Hamburg: Claassen & Goverts, 1957.
*Überallnie: Angsgewählte. Gedichte.* Munich, 1969.
*Dein Schweigen: Gedichte 1958–1961.* Hamburg: Claassen,
1962.
*Ein Wort weiter: Gedichte.* Hamburg: Claassen, 1965.
*Kein Zauberspruch.* Frankfurt: Insel, 1972.
Dagmar von Gersdorff. *Marie Luise Kaschnitz: Eine
Biographie.* Frankfurt, Insel, 1995.
*Sources in English*
Kaschnitz, Marie Louise. *Circe's Mountain: Stories By Marie
Luise Kaschnitz.* Lisel Mueller trans. Minneapolis, MN:
Milkweed Editions, 1990.
———. *Selected Later Poems of Marie Luise Kaschnitz.* Lisel
Mueller trans. Princeton, NJ: Princeton University Press,
1980.
*The House of Childhood,* Anni Whissen, trans.
Lincoln: University of Nebraska Press, 1990.
*Long Shadows.* Anni Whissen, trans. London, Ont.:
Moonstone Press, 1991.


HILDE DOMIN
*Originating Volumes*
*Hier: Gedichte.* Frankfurt am Main: S. Fischer, 1964.
Köln
Exil
*Nur eine Rose als Stütze.* Frankfurt am Main: S. Fischer, 1959.
Geburtstage
*Books by Hilde Domin in German*
*Nur eine Rose als Stütze.* Frankfurt am Main: S. Fischer, 1959.
*Rückkehr der Schiffe.* Frankfurt am Main: S. Fischer, 1962.
*Hier. Gedichte.* Frankfurt am Main: S. Fischer, 1964.
*Das zweite Paradies. Roman in Segmenten.* Munich: Piper,
1968.
*Ich will dich: Gedichte.* Munich: Piper, 1970.

*Wozu Lyrik heute?—Dichtung und Leser in der gesteuerten*
*Gesellschaft.* Munich: Piper, 1968.
*Von der Natur nicht vorgesehen. Autobiographisches.* Munich:
Piper, 1974.
*Aber die Hoffnung: Autobiographisches aus und über*
*Deutschland.* Munich: Piper, 1982.
*Gesammelte Gedichte.* Frankfurt am Main: S. Fischer, 1987.
*Nachkrieg und Unfrieden: Gedichte als Index 1945–1995.*
Hilde Domin and Clemens Greve, ed. Berlin: Neuweid a.
Rhein. Fischer (Tb.), Frankfurt: 1995.
*Sources in English*
McConnell, Robert G. *Hilde Domin: A Study in*
*Contemporary Poetry:* University of Toronto, 1966.
Stern, Dagmar C. *Hilde Domin:From Exile to Ideal:* Peter
Lang, 1980.
Stein, Agnes, ed. *Four German Poets: Günter Eich, Hilde*
*Domin, Erich Fried, Günter Kunert.* New York: Red Dust,
1980.


**DAGMAR NICK**
*Originating Volumes*
   *Zeugnis und Zeichen.* Munich: Delp'sche Verlagsbuchhandlung,
   1969.
      An Abel
      Den Generälen ins Soldbuch
      Aufruf
      Niemandsland
      Emigration
   *Gezählte Tage*, Gedichte Gebundene Ausgabe, 1986.
      Fluggenwetter
*Books by or about Dagmar Nick in German*
   *Märtyrer:* Gedichte. Verlag Katholisches Bibelwerk Stuttgart
   1947.
   *Das Buch des Holofernes:* Gedichte Freiburg/Br. Klemm, 1955.

*In Den Ellipsen Des Mondes: Gedichte*. Hamburg: Ellermann, 1959.

*Zeugnis und Zeichen* Munich: Delp'sche Verlagsbuchhandlung, 1969.

*Gezählte Tage. Gedichte*. Gebundene Ausgabe 1986.

*Wegmarken: Ausgewählte Gedichte*. Aachen: Rimbaud-Verlagsges, 2000.

*Liebesgedichte: von Dagmar Nick*. Aachen: Rimbaud-Verlagsges, 2001.

*Im Stillstand der Stunden: Gedichte*. Aachen: Rimbaud, 2001.

Friedrich, Sabine. *Traditionsbewusstsein als Lebensbewältigung: zu Leben und Werk der Dagmar Nick*. Frankurtam Main: P. Lang, 1990.

Sources in English

*Numbered Days*. Jim Barnes, trans. New Odyssey Press, 1998.

*Summons and Sign*. Jim Barnes, trans. Kirksville, MO: Chariton Review Press, 1980.

Dagmar Nick. *Lilith: A Metamorphosis*. Maren and David Partenheimer, trans. Kirksville, Mo.: Truman State University Press, 1995.

# FURTHER READING

Berman, Russell A. *Cultural Studies of Modern Germany: History, Representation, and Nationhood.* Madison: University of Wisconsin Press, 1994.

Cocalis, Susan L., ed. *German Feminist Poems from the Middle Ages to the Present: A Bilingual Anthology.* New York: Feminist Press, 1986.

Donahue, Neil H., and Doris Kirchner, eds. *Flight of Fantasy: New Perspectives on Inner Emigration in German Literature, 1933–1945.* New York: Berghahn Books, 2003.

Felstiner, John. *Paul Celan: Poet, Survivor, Jew.* New Haven, Conn.: Yale University Press, 1996.

Felstiner, Mary. *To Paint Her Life: Charlotte Salomon in the Nazi Era.* New York: Harper Collins, 1994.

Forster, Leonard, ed. *German Poetry 1944–1948.* Cambridge: Bowes & Bowes, 1949.

Frederiksen, Elke P., and Elizabeth G. Ametsbichler, eds. *Women Writers in German-Speaking Countries: A Bio-Bibliographical Critical Sourcebook.* Westport, Conn.: Greenwood, 1998.

Grimm, Reinhold, and Irmgard Elsner Hunt, eds. *German Twentieth Century Poetry.* New York: Continuum, 2001.

Hamburger, Michael, ed. *East German Poetry: An Anthology.* New York: Dutton, 1973.

———. *German Poetry, 1910–1975: An Anthology.* Manchester: Carcanet/New Press, 1977.

———. *A Proliferation of Prophets: Essays on German Writers from Nietzsche to Brecht.* New York: St. Martin's, 1983.

Hamburger, Michael, and Christopher Middleton, eds. *Modern German Poetry, 1910–1960: An Anthology with Verse Translations.* New York: Grove Press, 1962.

Ives, Rich, ed. *Evidence of Fire: An Anthology of Twentieth Century German Poetry.* Seattle, WA: Owl Creek Press, 1988.

Leeder, Karen. *Breaking Boundaries: A New Generation of Poets in the GDR.* Oxford: Clarendon Press, 1996.

Lorenz, Dagmar C. G. *Keepers of the Motherland: German Texts by Jewish Women Writers.* Lincoln: University of Nebraska Press, 1997.

Magris, Claudio. *Danube.* New York: Farrar, Straus, Giroux, 1989

Maley, Saundra Rose. *Solitary Apprenticeship: James Wright and German Poetry.* Distinguished Dissertations Series. Edwin Mellen Press, 1996.

Melin, Charlotte, ed. *German Poetry in Transition, 1945–1990.* Hanover, N.H., and London: University Press of New England, 1999.

Schwebell, Gertrude C., ed. *Contemporary German Poetry: An Anthology.* New York: New Directions, 1964.

Trakl, George. *Twenty Poems by George Trakl.* James Wright and Robert Bly, trans. Madison, Minn. The Sixties Press, 1961.

Zagajewski, Adam. *Two Cities: On Exile, History, and the Imagination.* Lillian Vallee, trans. Athens: University of Georgia Press, 2002.

# INDEX OF TITLES